Rx

For

FEAR

A Kingdom Prescription for Courage,
Clarity, and Emotional Freedom

Dr. Joke Solanke

Published by **Purpose and Pathway Publications**
All rights reserved worldwide.

Scripture quotations are taken from the **Holy Bible, New King James Version (NKJV)** and the **New Living Translation (NLT)**. Used by permission. All rights reserved.

First Edition: 2026
Printed in the United States of America

ISBNs
Paperback: 978-1-968717-13-1
eBook: 978-1-968717-14-8

Disclaimer

This book is intended for educational, inspirational, and informational purposes only. It is not intended to be a substitute for professional medical, psychological, legal, or financial advice, diagnosis, or treatment. Readers are encouraged to seek appropriate professional support when needed.

The author and publisher assume no responsibility or liability for the interpretation, application, or misuse of the information contained in this book.

Any references to real people, events, or situations are used solely for teaching and illustrative purposes. Names, identifying details, and circumstances have been altered where necessary to protect privacy.

DEDICATION

To all who have lived beneath fear's shadow and are ready to walk fully in truth, courage, and freedom.

TABLE OF CONTENTS

INTRODUCTION

Fear is not just an emotion—it is a system that must be dismantled.

R*x for Fear* is more than a book. The volume you hold in your hands is an evidence-based solution to one of humanity's oldest and most universal battles: the silent force that has crippled giants, paralyzed gifted minds, and caged destinies. It is intentionally designed as a journey of healing for the spirit, soul, and body. Every page functions as part of a treatment plan—a spiritual and psychological roadmap that empowers you to confront fear, decode its hidden mechanisms, and enter sustained freedom through the power of truth, renewal, and alignment.

Fear does not bow to avoidance—it bows to revelation. You cannot medicate fear into silence, nor suppress it into submission. Fear must be addressed with understanding, exposed by truth, and overthrown by divine authority. That is why every chapter has been structured like a prescription dose: a strategic blend of insight, Scripture, and guided reflection designed to bring healing to the places where fear has quietly lived, lingered, and limited destiny.

"For God has not given us the spirit of fear, but of power and of love and of a sound mind." — **2 Timothy 1:7 (NKJV)**

Fear is one of the most complex afflictions that has plagued humanity from the beginning. It infiltrates every dimension of human existence, yet it remains one of the least understood emotional and spiritual forces. In my years of patient care, I learned that fear is rarely recorded as a stand-alone diagnosis, yet it consistently hides behind many clinical conditions on mental health screenings. It is an equal-opportunity affliction; it respects no social class, race, education, or achievement. Fear has crippled kings and commoners alike.

Despite enormous scientific research into human behavior, no classification system has fully solved the riddle of fear as a singular condition. **ICD-10-CM** and **DSM-5** acknowledge fear indirectly—under anxiety, phobic disorders, nervousness, or worry. The absence of a direct diagnostic category reflects a deeper truth clinicians recognize from experience: fear is universal, yet elusive. It affects the body, mind, and spirit in ways that transcend medical coding.

As a clinician, I have seen fear manifest biologically through the nervous system as tremors, panic attacks, functional neurological symptoms, hyperventilation, and other forms of physiological distress. I have watched it manifest psychologically in the form of paranoia, obsessive-compulsive patterns, avoidance, and anxiety disorders. The body reacts, the mind obsesses, and the spirit withdraws. Fear hijacks the body's design for protection and turns it into a prison.

As a minister, I have seen fear disguise itself spiritually. It hides under religious language, perfectionism, hyper-responsibility, emotional withdrawal, or the need for extreme control. And as a human being, I have walked through seasons when fear whispered louder than faith.

One patient I will never forget was a police officer who sat in my office trembling. Her anxiety score was **21**, and her depression screening score was **27**. Tears flowed uncontrollably from someone trained to protect others—someone who believed she should never appear afraid. Behind the uniform was a woman suffocating under a weight she could not name. Clinically, we labeled her condition panic disorder and major depression. In truth, what I discerned beneath her symptoms was a spirit of fear—unseen, yet tormenting.

This book establishes fear as a foundational trigger in many mental and emotional battles.

Behind prolonged anxiety lies unresolved fear.

Behind depression rooted in hopelessness lies fear of the future or fear of inadequacy.

Behind trauma responses and PTSD lies fear encoded into memory.

Behind perfectionism lies fear of failure.

Behind impulsive control lies fear of chaos.

Behind avoidance lies fear of pain.

Every mental prison has a key, and more often than not, the lock holding that prison door closed is fear.

The Bible remains the only source that presents an antidote to fear that heals the whole person rather than numbing symptoms. The repeated instruction to **fear not** throughout Scripture functions as a daily prescription. The Designer of life knew fear would attack often, so He supplied truth often. Every "fear not" is a medicinal intervention. Every command to be courageous is a spiritual dose of restoration.

This book is that prescription. It is not motivational literature or inspirational consolation. It is a treatment plan for the spirit, the soul, and the body. Fear is not just an emotion; it is a system. It touches identity, decision-making, relationships, perception, confidence, and obedience. It locks gifts, silences voices, and sabotages destiny. It is subtle enough to look like wisdom, meekness, or logic while quietly draining courage from within.

Rx for Fear stands at the intersection of science and Scripture. It is not theory; it is therapy. It was born from the convergence of two worlds: the clinical marketplace and the Kingdom of revelation. Years of observing fear's patterns in patients, years of witnessing its effects in the church, and years of personal experience compelled this work. Every principle in this book has been tested by Scripture, proven by experience, and anchored in grace.

Because fear affects the whole person, healing must reach the whole person as well. Throughout these pages, you will experience transformation on multiple levels at the same time. Your spirit will receive truth and revelation that dismantle the lies and spiritual intrusions that give fear its authority. Your soul—your thoughts, emotions, and relational patterns—will be guided into regulation and renewal so that perception and decision-making are no longer controlled by anxiety or insecurity. And your body will participate in that healing journey as you learn how fear influences the nervous system, hormones, sleep, and physical stability, and how practices such as worship, prayer, journaling, silence, and deep rest restore physiological peace.

When the spirit, soul, and body heal together, fear loses the ability to return. Transformation becomes sustainable rather than temporary. You are not just learning about fear—you are being equipped to live free from it.

Each chapter in this book functions like a dose of treatment. Through biblical portraits of men and women who encountered fear in its rawest form, you will observe how fear enters, how it grows, and how it can be dismantled. You will be guided to diagnose its tactics, recognize its disguises, interrupt its patterns, and rebuild emotional and spiritual resilience until courage rises naturally again. What begins as insight will become empowerment. What begins as revelation will become renewal.

Read slowly. Reflect deeply. Allow the process to do its work. Every chapter includes clinical insights, biblical illumination, and activation steps designed to bring healing to places where fear has been normalized for too long.

This is not theory. It is divine therapy. The Spirit of God is your Counselor, your Comforter, and your Physician.

Let each page be a dose of light, clarity, courage, and peace until emotional freedom becomes your new normal—and the Spirit of power, love, and a sound mind becomes your permanent identity.

Welcome to your prescription for healing. Welcome to courage, clarity, peace, and wholeness. Welcome to *Rx for Fear*.

CHAPTER 1

Understanding the Dynamics of Fear: Spirit, Soul, and Body

Fear can live in the body, hide in the soul, and whisper in the spirit. To defeat it, you must understand how it operates in all three.

> *"My heart is severely pained within me,*
> *And the terrors of death have fallen upon me.*
> *Fearfulness and trembling have come upon me,*
> *And horror has overwhelmed me."* — **Psalm 55:4–5 (NKJV)**

To those familiar with the life of David—the shepherd, warrior, psalmist, and king—these words carry profound weight. David was not a timid man. He faced lions and bears in solitude, confronted Goliath in public, led armies into battle, and ruled a nation with divine favor. Yet the same man who ran toward giants also wrote about paralyzing fear—more than once.

This tells us something essential: fear can creep in at any time, regardless of who you are or what victories you have achieved. It visits prophets and professionals, soldiers and scholars, believers and doubters alike. Fear respects neither title nor anointing—it is an equalizer of human experience.

And perhaps that is why David's honesty is so relatable. A man after God's own heart admits, "fearfulness and trembling have come upon me." He exposes what many of us hide: moments of greatness do not exempt us from moments of weakness.

Fear in Real Life

She was well dressed and articulate. Her visit to my clinic was for what she described as a hormonal imbalance—one of those patients who arrive with a self-diagnosis and hope you will simply write the prescription they have already chosen.

I listened politely, but—as I always do—looked beyond the presenting complaint. I insisted on hearing her story in full so I could form a true differential diagnosis. As she spoke, I recommended a standard anxiety and depression screening. She hesitated—almost offended. In her mind, a Christian could not possibly be depressed.

I promised to order the labs she wanted to rule out endocrine causes, but I continued the conversation with gentle honesty.

"You are severely depressed," I said softly. "You have mastered the art of normalizing your abnormalities. You have become proficient in hiding your fears. The only reason you are here today is because you have reached the limit of adaptation and are searching for a respectable diagnosis to hide under."

She looked at me intently, then tears began to fall. That moment became the beginning of her liberation. As predicted, every lab was normal. The problem was not in her hormones—it was in her heart.

Another patient—let's call her Patient B—was more forthcoming. She openly described her distress as PTSD and anxiety. Her fear was crippling. Once, on her way to an appointment, she had to pull to the side of the road because her hands trembled so violently she could not drive. Medication offered temporary relief but quickly lost efficacy; doses needed constant adjustment.

All neurological exams and imaging were normal. I discerned what the data could not confirm: she was under bondage to fear—the kind Scripture calls tormenting. It came in waves—sometimes dormant, then suddenly rising to overshadow her like a storm that paralyzes even the will to function.

Two women, two faces of the same reality—one disguising fear beneath intellect and achievement, the other drowning under its visible grip. Both reveal a truth rarely emphasized in medical training: fear is not only emotional; it is spiritual. It infiltrates physiology, distorts cognition, and imprisons the soul.

Many of us grew up verbalizing fear with no guidance on how to confront it. In some cultures, fear was even used to control—invoking darkness or imagined creatures to force obedience. Small wonder darkness remains one of humanity's oldest triggers; where there is illumination, fear loses one of its greatest advantages.

The First Mention of Fear

The first time fear appears in Scripture is **Genesis 3:10**. After Adam and Eve ate from the forbidden tree, they hid from God. When God called, "Where are you?" Adam replied:

"I heard Your voice in the garden, and I was afraid because I was naked; and I hid myself." — **Genesis 3:10 (NKJV)**

Fear entered human consciousness the moment disobedience severed fellowship with God. What began as divine intimacy turned into hiding—evidence that fear is the first emotional symptom of spiritual separation.

The first time God said, "Do not be afraid," was **Genesis 15:1**:

"After these things the word of the Lord came to Abram in a vision, saying, 'Do not be afraid, Abram. I am your shield, your exceedingly great reward.'" — **Genesis 15:1 (NKJV)**

Between Adam's hiding and Abram's reassurance lies humanity's struggle with fear—and God's consistent invitation to trust. Fear entered through disconnection; peace is restored through relationship.

We will unpack Eden's moment and Abram's promise in Chapter 2. First, we must define what fear is and how it operates today—in the body, the mind, and the unseen places of the heart.

What Is Fear?

Fear wears many faces. It speaks the language of science, psychology, philosophy, and theology—and yet no single field fully explains it.

A biologist may call it a survival response. A psychologist may call it a conditioned emotion. A philosopher may call it the anticipation of loss. But Scripture goes deeper: it identifies fear as a spiritual force.

Each definition captures a fragment of truth; none alone reveals the whole. Fear is both seen and unseen, felt and transferred. It moves through body chemistry, shapes thought patterns, and influences decisions—yet its deepest roots are spiritual.

The Scientific Lens

The Body's Reaction

Biologically, fear is a neurochemical reaction that mobilizes the body when danger is perceived. The amygdala sounds the alarm; adrenaline and cortisol surge; the heart rate spikes; pupils dilate; blood is redirected to the muscles. This "fight-or-flight" response can save a life in a true emergency.

The paradox is this: what protects physically can destroy emotionally when constantly activated. Chronic fear keeps the body in survival mode long after danger is gone—exhausting the heart, weakening immunity, disrupting sleep, and stealing rest. Science can trace the mechanism, but not the meaning. It can measure what the body does, but it cannot fully explain why the soul feels unsafe when no threat is present.

The Psychological Lens

The Mind's Interpretation

Psychology defines fear as an emotional and cognitive response to perceived danger. Perception is pivotal. Two people can face the same moment—one panics, the other rests—because fear is as much about interpretation as pressure.

Fear can be acute (sudden and intense), chronic (subtle and ongoing), or existential (related to meaning or mortality). The mind stores fear through conditioning: a bite from one dog becomes fear of all dogs; a betrayal becomes global distrust. Therapy can reframe patterns, yet many still feel bound—because the mind can be trained by reason, but the spirit is restored by truth.

The Philosophical Lens

The Soul's Struggle for Control

Philosophers have called fear the anticipation of pain and the tension of human freedom. Modern thought often views fear as the cost of awareness—the struggle between what we can control and what we cannot. We may rename fear as caution or realism; in doing so, we normalize what God never intended to be normal. Fear becomes so common that peace feels like a luxury instead of a promise.

The Biblical Lens

The Spirit's Disconnection

Scripture speaks with clarity:

"For God has not given us a spirit of fear, but of power and of love and of a sound mind." — **2 Timothy 1:7 (NKJV)**

Fear is not merely a feeling; it is identified as a spirit—an intruder that gains influence wherever truth is absent. Fear thrives where fellowship is broken—first with God, then with self, and finally with others. It replaces trust with torment, confidence with confusion, and peace with panic.

This is why Scripture does not teach us to manage fear as a permanent resident. It teaches us to cast it out:

"There is no fear in love; but perfect love casts out fear, because fear involves torment." — **1 John 4:18 (NKJV)**

Where truth is absent, lies take root. Where light is dim, shadows grow. Where God's voice is ignored, fear becomes loud.

Defining Fear

To address fear effectively, we must define it accurately.

Fear is a **response**, a **condition**, and a **spirit**—a threefold reality that touches every dimension of human existence.

- **As a response**, fear is the body's automatic reaction to perceived danger. It is part of the fight–flight–freeze mechanism.

- **As a condition**, fear becomes distortion when it persists beyond genuine threat. It magnifies risk, minimizes truth, and hardens into hypervigilance, anxiety disorders, phobias, or compulsions.

- **As a spirit**, fear is a spiritual force that manipulates perception and disrupts faith. Scripture names it plainly: the spirit of fear (2 Timothy 1:7). It gains access through disconnection from divine truth. It speaks to the mind, feeds on insecurity, and produces torment in the absence of faith.

Put plainly:

Fear is disordered awareness of danger that originates spiritually, expresses psychologically, and manifests physiologically.

It begins in the spirit as disconnection from truth, is processed in the soul as distorted thought, and is experienced in the body as distress and dysfunction. Fear is the first psychosomatic-spiritual disease of mankind—one condition affecting awareness, emotion, and physiology at once.

The Spirit–Soul–Body Connection

"Now may the God of peace Himself sanctify you completely; and may your whole spirit, soul, and body be preserved blameless at the coming of our Lord Jesus Christ." — **1 Thessalonians 5:23 (NKJV)**

Human beings are triune—spirit, soul, and body. Fear interacts with each dimension differently, yet simultaneously.

In the spirit (the root)

Fear begins as spiritual disconnection. When the spirit is misaligned with its Creator, awareness shifts from faith to self-preservation. Divine perspective is lost. Adam's first fear was not of a beast or a storm—it was of God's presence. When intimacy breaks, fear finds room to grow.

In the soul (the voice)

The soul—thoughts, emotions, and will—becomes a battlefield. Fear speaks as worry, hesitation, self-doubt, and inner conflict. If unchecked, these narratives harden into beliefs: *I am not enough. It will not work. I am unsafe.*

In the body (the expression)

The body becomes the visible stage for an invisible war. Stress hormones elevate heart rate, suppress immunity, disrupt digestion, and damage sleep. The amygdala sounds the alarm, the hypothalamus coordinates the stress cascade, and the prefrontal cortex (reason) can go temporarily offline. People say or do irrational things because fear alters function. Chronic fear can even reinforce anxiety loops through repeated neurological patterns.

Fear as a Spiritual Disorder

Because fear originates in the spirit, approaches that ignore the spiritual root tend to manage symptoms without restoring wholeness. Medication may calm the body. Therapy may reframe the mind. Only truth liberates the spirit.

Scripture does not merely advise "do not fear"; it replaces fear with faith through relationship and revelation. Every "fear not" is both command and cure—a prescription from the Designer who understands the design.

Bridge: This is why fear must be confronted at the level it begins, not only at the level it shows. What you tolerate in the unseen will eventually manifest in the seen.

Chapter 1 Reflection

Understanding the Dynamics of Fear: Spirit, Soul & Body

"For God has not given us a spirit of fear, but of power and of love and of a sound mind."
— 2 Timothy 1:7 (NKJV)

Awareness

Where do you most often experience fear—internally in your thoughts, emotionally in your reactions, or physically in your body? What symptoms or patterns have you normalized?

Insight

What did this chapter reveal about how fear operates simultaneously in the spirit, soul, and body rather than as a single emotional experience?

Alignment

Which truth from Scripture in this chapter corrects how you have interpreted fear—especially the truth that fear is not from God?

Action

What intentional step will you take to interrupt fear's influence in one area of your life (spiritual, emotional, or physical) this week?

Declaration

"I refuse to normalize fear. My spirit aligns with truth, my soul is renewed by faith, and my body responds to peace. I live governed by clarity, courage, and divine order."

CHAPTER 2

The Genesis of Fear

"Fear does not stop death. It stops life."

"And I heard Your voice in the garden, and I was afraid because I was naked; and I hid myself."
— *Genesis 3:10 (NKJV)*

One of the foundational principles in solving medical problems is understanding root cause. In clinical science, we call it **root-cause analysis**—the process of tracing symptoms back to their origin so that treatment addresses the disease, not merely its manifestations. In business and psychology, we call it **problem identification**—the discipline of naming the true issue before creating a solution.

Lasting healing—whether physical, emotional, or spiritual—is impossible without an accurate diagnosis. A misdiagnosed condition will always lead to mistreatment. In the same way, to address fear effectively, we must identify where it began, how it evolved, and why it persists.

This book does not introduce a new cure; it presents an ancient prescription that has always existed but is often misunderstood or ignored. The goal is to make that divine solution practical—an approach that integrates faith, insight, and daily living. The aim is not discovery, but clarity: to reveal what has always been true—**God already provided a remedy for fear.**

This chapter begins with the first documented case of fear—the moment it entered human consciousness. In the chapters that follow, we will examine men and women in Scripture who battled fear in its many forms and learn how they either managed it or overcame it. By the end of this journey, we will arrive at a practical framework—what, in clinical terms, could be compared to an evidence-based plan—for conquering fear and walking in peace.

So how did fear begin? It started in the garden, with Adam and Eve—at the moment intimacy with God shifted into intimidation within man.

When Intimacy Turned Into Intimidation

The Shift Was in Man, Not in God

Before the fall, Adam and Eve lived in harmony with God. His presence was their atmosphere. His voice was their comfort. Their awareness of Him produced peace, not panic. Their nakedness represented innocence, not shame. They knew no fear because they knew no separation.

But when disobedience entered, their perception changed—not God's posture. What had always been intimate suddenly felt intimidating—not because God became a threat, but because guilt distorted their awareness of His nature. The same presence that once brought joy now evoked discomfort. The same voice that once signaled communion now sounded like confrontation.

Sin did not change who God was; it changed what humanity saw. The light of His glory now revealed what they wished to hide. The holiness that once covered them now exposed them. Fear was born the moment **self-awareness replaced God-awareness.**

Adam's fear was not rooted in divine anger—it was rooted in internal disconnection. He was not fleeing from judgment, but from exposure. Fear emerged when the human heart could no longer interpret divine love correctly.

This is the essence of spiritual distortion: when what is meant to heal begins to feel harmful, and what was designed to draw us near seems to push us away.

Bridge: To understand fear, we must follow the pathway it took. Genesis gives us a sequence—simple, but clinically precise.

The Sequence of Separation

- **Disobedience** — breaking divine instruction.
- **Distortion** — twisting perception.
- **Disconnection** — losing spiritual alignment.
- **Dread** — experiencing the emotional consequence.

Adam's statement, *"I was afraid because I was naked,"* reveals the anatomy of separation. His fear was not primarily about punishment; it was about exposure. The problem was not that God had withdrawn—the problem was that man could no longer stand unveiled before Him. Fear is the soul's instinctive response to the loss of covering.

What Adam felt is what we feel whenever trust is broken—the terror of being uncovered, unprotected, and alone. Fear, then, is not merely an emotion; it is the emotional language of spiritual exile.

The Psychology of Hiding

When fear enters, hiding follows. Humanity's reflex to conceal is not only psychological—it is spiritual and physiological. The amygdala triggers retreat, the soul hides through avoidance, and the spirit withdraws from divine dialogue.

We hide behind many things: work, intellect, religion, perfectionism, or even a diagnosis—anything that makes us feel "covered" again. But coverings without confession only deepen separation.

God's first question to humanity was not, "What have you done?" but *"Where are you?"* (Genesis 3:9). It was not an interrogation—it was an invitation. While fear pushes us away from presence, love calls us back into it.

Bridge: In that one moment, Adam shifted from faith to self-preservation. That transition still explains much of modern anxiety.

The First Fear Response

From Faith to Self-Preservation

Adam's declaration—*"I was afraid because I was naked"*—*marks humanity's first transition from dependence on divine protection to the burden of self-protection. Before sin, Adam's security was relational; after sin, it became situational. This is the root of many anxieties: the weight of survival without the assurance of presence.

Fear is not merely the absence of courage—it is the absence of awareness of God.

Where faith says, *"The Lord is my light and my salvation; whom shall I fear?"* (Psalm 27:1), fear says, "I must protect myself, for I am alone."

This is why fear is exhausting: it demands that we become our own savior.

The Divine Diagnosis

God's gentle question—*"Where are you?"*—was a divine diagnostic test. He was not seeking information; He was revealing condition. His next questions follow the pattern of assessment:

- *"Who told you that you were naked?"* — exposes the source of distorted awareness.

- *"Have you eaten…?"* — identifies the door that was opened.

These questions unveil the true pathology of fear: separation from truth. Before God ever judged humanity, He asked questions designed to restore awareness. Every divine question is an invitation to healing.

Fear's Inheritance

From that moment, fear became generational. Humanity carried the echo of Eden's disconnection. We are born seeking safety and spend our lives trying to feel covered—physically, emotionally, and spiritually. Many patterns of anxiety, control, and perfectionism whisper the same confession Adam made: "I was afraid."

But even in that moment of loss, God revealed His cure. Before Adam left the garden, the Lord clothed him with garments of skin—a prophetic symbol of redemption, pointing to the day when blood would cover what shame exposed.

Fear began in the garden, but so did grace.

Fear began as a symptom of disconnection, not danger. It is not proof that God has abandoned us—it is evidence that we have lost awareness of Him.

The Threefold Manifestation of Fear

"And I heard Your voice in the garden, and I was afraid because I was naked; and I hid myself." — **Genesis 3:10 (NKJV)**

This single verse contains the anatomy of fear. In one statement, Adam describes its spiritual, psychological, and physical dimensions— the threefold manifestation that still governs human experience today.

1. "I heard Your voice in the garden" — The Spiritual Reaction

The spirit recognizes the presence of God, but guilt distorts perception. The same voice that once comforted him now feels convicting. What changed was not God's tone but Adam's awareness. Fear begins here—not merely as emotion, but as spiritual distortion, when revelation is replaced by misinterpretation.

When we lose awareness of divine love, even holiness can feel hostile. The spirit, once attuned to communion, now trembles at the sound of truth.

2. "I was afraid because I was naked" — The Psychological and Emotional Reaction

The soul translates spiritual distortion into emotion. Nakedness becomes symbolic of vulnerability—the awareness of exposure and inadequacy. What was once innocence now feels unsafe. Shame enters as the soul's attempt to process separation: "I am unworthy. I am unprotected. I am alone."

Fear here takes the form of insecurity, overthinking, and the emotional narrative of insufficiency.

3. "I hid myself" — The Physical Reaction

Finally, the body expresses what the soul feels. Adam's retreat mirrors humanity's instinct to avoid, conceal, and withdraw. Physiologically, this is the fight, flight, or freeze response: adrenaline surges, cortisol rises, and the body prepares to defend against perceived threat.

In a single sentence, Adam gives the first "clinical note" of fear in human history. Fear is not one-dimensional; it is a cascading disorder of awareness that begins in the spirit, filters through the soul, and expresses itself in the body.

When the spirit disconnects from truth, the soul loses peace, and the body loses rest.

The Anatomy of Separation

How Fear Rewires the Soul and the Brain

When Adam and Eve hid, something deeper than emotion occurred. Separation from God did not only affect their spiritual condition; it altered the rhythm of their inner world. Fear did not remain in the garden—it entered the nervous system of humanity.

The fall introduced fragmentation: the spirit lost alignment with God, the soul became reactive, and the body learned survival mode. What was once harmony became disorder.

1. The Soul: Where Separation Is Felt

The soul—the seat of thought, emotion, and will—became the first battlefield after the fall. In disconnection, the mind began to replay danger even when none existed. Memory became colored by insecurity; imagination became dominated by threat.

This is why Scripture speaks to the soul as needing restoration: *"Why are you cast down, O my soul? ... Hope in God."* — **Psalm 42:11 (NKJV)**

Without divine communion, the soul develops compensatory mechanisms—control, perfectionism, avoidance—to create a false sense of safety.

Modern psychology calls this hypervigilance; Scripture calls it toiling.

2. The Brain: Where Fear Leaves Its Imprint

Neuroscience confirms what Scripture revealed first: fear alters perception and function. The amygdala becomes hypersensitive under chronic stress. The hypothalamus signals a cascade of stress hormones—adrenaline and cortisol—preparing the body for defense. At the same time, the prefrontal cortex (reason and decision-making) can be subdued by survival instinct. This is why fear can hijack judgment.

Repeated exposure to fear creates neurological grooves—pathways that make it easier to panic and harder to rest. Clinically, this is evident in anxiety disorders, trauma responses, and obsessive thought cycles.

Scripture describes the experience plainly:
"Fear involves torment." — **1 John 4:18 (NKJV)**

Torment is ongoing agitation—alarm without relief.

3. The Spirit: Where Healing Must Begin

While science can trace the mechanism, only Scripture explains the meaning. Fear is more than chemistry; it is evidence of disconnection. The human spirit was created to receive safety through relationship with God. When that connection is disrupted, the system compensates: the brain signals danger, the soul searches for control, and the body bears symptoms.

This is why medical and psychological interventions, though valuable, cannot by themselves produce full restoration. Medication may calm the body. Therapy can renew thought patterns. But only truth realigns the spirit.

What Scripture calls **"the renewing of your mind"** is observable transformation.
"And do not be conformed to this world, but be transformed by the renewing of your mind…" — **Romans 12:2 (NKJV)**

4. The Hidden Cost of Separation

Fear's greatest damage is not trembling—it is distortion. It redefines how we see God, ourselves, and others. Under fear's influence, love feels risky, rest feels irresponsible, and surrender feels unsafe. The person begins to live in defense, expending energy on survival rather than purpose.

Every chronic fear is a form of spiritual amnesia—forgetting who God is and who we are in Him.

5. The Way Back: Reconnection Restores Regulation

God's first prescription for fear was not a technique—it was presence. Before He clothed Adam, He called to him. Before He corrected behavior, He pursued relationship.

Divine proximity regulates the human system. When the spirit reconnects with its Source, the soul finds peace and the body finds rhythm. Prayer, worship, meditation on Scripture, and communion with God are not empty rituals; they are spiritual and neurological recalibrations.

"You will keep him in perfect peace, whose mind is stayed on You, because he trusts in You."— **Isaiah 26:3 (NKJV)**

Peace is not the absence of problems; it is the presence of proper alignment.

Chapter 2 Reflection — The Genesis of Fear

"I heard Your voice in the garden, and I was afraid because
I was naked; and I hid myself."
— Genesis 3:10 (NKJV)

Fear did not begin as a threat in the environment; it began as a fracture in awareness. This chapter reveals that fear enters when God-awareness is replaced by self-protection. Healing begins when alignment is restored.

Awareness Question

Where did fear first enter your story—not merely as an emotion, but as a shift in trust, perception, or spiritual awareness?

Insight Question

In what ways has fear caused you to hide—through control, avoidance, performance, or self-protection—rather than remain present with God?

Alignment Question

Which part of you is currently most affected by fear—your spirit (distance from God), your soul (distorted thoughts or emotions), or your body (stress responses and physical symptoms)?

Action Question

What intentional step will you take this week to restore God-awareness in place of self-preservation—through prayer, Scripture meditation, stillness, worship, or honest confession?

Declaration

Fear did not originate in me, and it does not govern me. I return to God-awareness. My spirit is aligned with truth, my soul is restored by faith, and my body rests in divine peace. I refuse to hide. I walk uncovered, unashamed, and secure in His presence.

CHAPTER 3

Fear of the Unknown — Moses and the Call to Destiny

> *"Then Moses said to God, 'Who am I that I should go to Pharaoh and that I should bring the children of Israel out of Egypt?'"* — **Exodus 3:11 (NKJV)**

We've seen from history how Moses' life unfolded—and how some may relate to his unique opportunities and hidden fears. He was a child of providence, miraculously preserved when others were massacred. He grew up under the grace of exemption—spared from slavery, hunger, and hardship. While his people languished in oppression, he lived in privilege. He attended the best schools, received elite training, and moved confidently among royalty.

Moses once spoke with boldness and carried himself with certainty—until life happened. An unexpected event on the blind side of destiny altered everything. The man who once defended justice became a fugitive. A single act of anger, an unplanned outburst, sent him running into exile. There, in the wilderness, trauma rewrote his identity. The eloquent prince became a hesitant shepherd; the bold liberator became a fearful wanderer.

He had known power—but not purpose. He had tasted privilege—but not peace. And now, the weight of guilt, failure, and regret pressed heavily upon his soul.

Fear can enter through failure but live through guilt.

Moses' fear was not merely of Pharaoh—it was of himself. He feared his own weakness, his own shadow, his own history. He feared returning to the place where he lost control. What modern psychology might label post-traumatic stress, Scripture reveals as spiritual fracture—the inner wound that distorts perception and limits obedience.

Every time something threatened to strip away his adapted security, the old terror resurfaced. Like many who suppress unresolved pain, Moses learned to function within fear rather than conquer it. Yet when God appeared to him at the burning bush, the conversation exposed every suppressed insecurity:

- "Who am I?" — the fear of inadequacy.
- "What if they don't believe me?" — the fear of rejection.
- "I am not eloquent." — the fear of failure.
- "Please send someone else." — the fear of responsibility.

These were not excuses—they were echoes of trauma. Each statement revealed a layer of his fractured self-image.

Fear often hides beneath logic; it sounds rational but roots in pain.

Moses' story reminds us that destiny does not exempt us from fear—it exposes it. Every divine call awakens both purpose and resistance, for the same God who calls us also confronts what paralyzes us. The journey of healing begins when we allow God to speak not only to our assignment but also to our anxiety.

Bridge: This is why the burning bush is not only a call to ministry—it is a call to inner restoration. Before Moses could confront Pharaoh outwardly, he had to face fear inwardly.

The Framework of Fear

Eight Pillars Revealed in Moses' Journey

"And I heard Your voice in the garden, and I was afraid because I was naked; and I hid myself." — **Genesis 3:10 (NKJV)**

"Who am I that I should go to Pharaoh...?" — **Exodus 3:11 (NKJV)**

"O my Lord, please send by the hand of whomever else You may send." — **Exodus 4:13 (NKJV)**

Fear does not appear suddenly; it constructs itself through experience, thought, and disconnection. Each layer reinforces the next, forming an invisible system that governs reaction, perception, and belief. To dismantle fear, we must understand its framework—the eight pillars that keep it standing. Moses' life gives us a vivid case study of this architecture in motion.

1. Guilt — The Weight of What Was

Moses carried the hidden weight of guilt from the day he killed the Egyptian (Exodus 2:12). Although his motive was justice, his method violated divine order. He buried the body in the sand—a physical act that symbolized his first attempt to bury guilt beneath silence.

Guilt says: "I did wrong, therefore I must hide."

Clinically, guilt manifests as internal agitation—restlessness of the mind that revisits the scene again and again. Spiritually, it is the inability to receive forgiveness because the soul still identifies with the act. For Moses, guilt rewrote his confidence. The man who once stood up for others could no longer stand before himself.

2. Shame — The Fear of Exposure

When guilt is not confessed, it evolves into shame. Shame changes the inner narrative from "I did wrong" to "I am wrong." Moses' years in Midian were years of internal exile—not just from Egypt but from identity. The prince became a shepherd. The leader became invisible.

"Then Moses fled from the face of Pharaoh and dwelt in the land of Midian; and he sat down by a well." — **Exodus 2:15 (NKJV)**

Shame convinced him that his failure disqualified him permanently. It is the same psychological mechanism that drives many into withdrawal—a false peace built on avoidance.

Shame says: "You are your past." But grace says: "Your past is what I redeem."

3. Failure — The Fear of Trying Again

Failure was Moses' greatest tormentor. He had once tried to be a deliverer and failed catastrophically. That memory became his internal regulator—the subconscious vow that said, "Never again." When God called him to return to Egypt, the flashbacks of failure were louder than the voice of faith.

"Who am I that I should go...?" — **Exodus 3:11 (NKJV)**

Clinically, failure can create avoidance conditioning—a reflexive shutdown whenever a situation resembles past pain. Spiritually, it's the erosion of expectancy. Failure made Moses second-guess even his calling.

Failure says: "I've tried before; I won't survive another loss."

4. Helplessness — The Fear of Powerlessness

Helplessness is the child of failure. When effort no longer seems to change outcome, the soul resigns. Moses' protest—"I am not eloquent" (Exodus 4:10)—reveals more than speech insecurity. It shows a man convinced he no longer has agency.

Psychologically, this aligns with learned helplessness, where repeated trauma convinces a person that action is futile. Spiritually, it reflects unbelief—the conviction that even with God's help, nothing will work.

Helplessness says: "I can't." Faith whispers: "You never had to—I will."

5. Control — The Fear of Uncertainty

Fear's favorite disguise is control. Moses' early act of killing the Egyptian (Exodus 2:12) was born out of righteous anger—but also the need to control an outcome God had not yet authorized. When fear of injustice meets impatience, control becomes the counterfeit of trust. Control is an anxious attempt to manage divine timing.

Clinically, control manifests as hypervigilance—the mind's attempt to predict and prevent all possible harm. Spiritually, it is a subtle form of pride—dependence on self wrapped in the language of responsibility.

Control says: "If I don't fix it, it will fail."
Trust says: *"Be still, and know that I am God."* — **Psalm 46:10 (NKJV)**

6. Insecurity — The Fear of Insufficiency

Insecurity is the internal argument between calling and confidence. When Moses said, "I am not eloquent... I am slow of speech" (Exodus 4:10), he wasn't only describing a limitation—he was confessing identity distortion. Years of wilderness silence had muted the prince's voice. Insecurity made him measure his worth by his weakness.

Clinically, insecurity presents as impostor syndrome—the belief that one's role exceeds one's worth. Spiritually, it manifests as doubt in divine wisdom: "God, You picked the wrong person."

Insecurity says: "I'm not enough." Grace says: "I AM is with you."

7. Anxiety — The Fear of the Future

Anxiety is fear projected forward. Even after God assured him, Moses' mind fixated on what could go wrong: "What if they do not believe me?" (Exodus 4:1). This anticipatory fear kept him analyzing outcomes rather than accepting assurance.

Clinically, anxiety engages the amygdala, flooding the body with stress hormones even in safety. Spiritually, it reveals a subtle mistrust in divine sovereignty. Anxiety replaces "what God said" with "what if."

Anxiety says: "The future is uncertain." Faith responds: "The future is secure in His hands."

8. Isolation — The Fear of Connection

Isolation is fear's final fortress. After years of disappointment, Moses found safety in solitude. He married, had children, tended sheep—but withdrew from destiny. When God called, his reflex was not rebellion but reluctance:

"O my Lord, please send by the hand of whomever else You may send."
— **Exodus 4:13 (NKJV)**

Isolation feels safe because it minimizes risk. But spiritually, it starves destiny. God's remedy was relational—He sent Aaron to join him (Exodus 4:14). Healing came through partnership, not independence.

Isolation says: "I'm safer alone."
Purpose says: *"It is not good that man should be alone."* — **Genesis 2:18 (NKJV)**

The Pattern of Fear in Moses' Life

If you look closely, each pillar of fear in Moses' story follows a divine invitation:

- Guilt and shame entered after his failure.

- Helplessness and control emerged in his exile.

- Insecurity and anxiety surfaced at his calling.

- Isolation marked his avoidance of the mission.

Yet God's presence dismantled them one by one—not by power, but by proximity. Every time Moses said, "I can't," God responded, "I will."

"Certainly I will be with you." — **Exodus 3:12 (NKJV)**

Fear is not eradicated by courage but displaced by presence. God never answered Moses' fears with logic—He answered them with Himself.

Bridge: This is the turning point: Moses did not need a new personality. He needed a new awareness of Presence. What fear had fractured, communion would restore.

The Psychology of the Call

When God Speaks to a Wounded Mind

"And the Angel of the Lord appeared to him in a flame of fire from the midst of a bush. So he looked, and behold, the bush was burning with fire, but the bush was not consumed." — **Exodus 3:2 (NKJV)**

The conversation between God and Moses at the burning bush is far more than a call to leadership; it is a divine therapy session—a sacred dialogue between the Creator and a man wounded by failure, fear, and time. For years, Moses lived in silence. His geography changed, but his psychology remained fractured. The fire that once symbolized passion and justice had dimmed into guarded caution. When God reignited the flame, Moses' first response was not excitement—it was anxiety. The same fire that once consumed him with zeal now reminded him of everything that had gone wrong.

Healing often begins at the site of our last defeat.

God did not introduce something new at the burning bush—He revisited something unresolved. The bush burned but was not consumed. That was the therapy in motion. It was a visual parable: "You can burn again and not be destroyed this time." God was showing Moses that the same passion which once led to failure could now be refined by divine fire. The fire was not punishment—it was purification.

God's Healing Approach: A Divine Counseling Model

Every statement God made followed a distinct therapeutic progression. He addressed the psychological, emotional, and spiritual dimensions of Moses' fear one layer at a time.

First, Recognition: God called him personally—"Moses, Moses." Before purpose could be restored, identity had to be reawakened. By calling his name twice, God stabilized a fragmented mind. In trauma therapy, this is called grounding—helping the individual return to present awareness. Spiritually, God was saying, "You are still who I called you to be, even after what you've become." Fear fragments identity; God restores it through recognition.

Second, Reframing: "Take your sandals off your feet, for the place where you stand is holy ground." God shifted Moses from the ordinary to the sacred. He redefined his environment—not as exile but as encounter. In counseling terms, this is reframing: changing the meaning attached to pain. Spiritually, it marked the moment when wilderness turned into holy ground. Revelation begins when we stop calling our wilderness punishment and start calling it preparation.

Third, Reassurance: Before instruction came validation. God said, "I have surely seen... I have heard... I know... I have come down." Those statements formed the language of divine empathy. God entered Moses' story emotionally before engaging him missionally. This was trauma-informed care in its purest form—He acknowledged the wound before applying the call. The God who sends you is the same God who first studies your scars.

Fourth, Recommissioning: After healing came purpose. "Come now, therefore, and I will send you." This was not an invitation to relive Egypt's trauma—it was a call to redeem it. Moses' mission would now become the medicine for his past. But before he could accept it, every buried fear surfaced again, each one disguised as logic.

The Dialogue of Fear and Faith

Each objection Moses raised was not rebellion—it was revelation of a wounded psyche.

- When he said, "Who am I?", it exposed his fear of inadequacy. God replied, "I will be with you." Presence, not perfection, is the cure for insecurity.

- When he asked what to say, it revealed his fear of legitimacy. God answered with His own Name—divine identity covering human deficiency.

- When he said, "What if they will not believe me?", it revealed the fear of rejection. God gave him signs—evidence that truth would outrun intimidation.

- When he confessed, "I am not eloquent," it showed his fear of exposure. God reminded him that the Creator of the mouth can reclaim the voice fear silenced.

- And when Moses pleaded, "Please send someone else," it revealed the fear of responsibility. God answered with provision—Aaron as companion. Healing came through connection, not isolation.

Each divine response dismantled one psychological stronghold at a time. God did not shame Moses for his hesitation—He restructured his internal narrative through truth and presence. Fear thrives on false perception; healing begins when truth reclaims interpretation.

The Healing Sequence

The process God used with Moses is still His method today. It moves through four sacred stages:

1. **Recognition** — God calls your name, reconnecting you with identity.

2. **Reframing** — He redefines your environment, revealing divine purpose in painful places.

3. **Reassurance** — He validates your pain before assigning new responsibility.

4. **Recommissioning** — He sends you forward, not as who you were, but as who He has healed.

This is the divine order of recovery: healing the mind, renewing the heart, and restoring destiny through relationship, not reprimand. God doesn't erase history—He redeems it.

Clinical Parallels and Spiritual Integration

Moses' journey mirrors the stages of trauma recovery familiar in modern psychology. In clinical practice, the process begins with grounding (awareness of self), moves into cognitive restructuring (changing thought patterns), continues with validation (empathic acknowledgment), and culminates in behavioral activation (restored action and purpose).

Spiritually, these correspond to God's model of transformation: recognition, reframing, reassurance, and recommissioning. Both systems—clinical and divine—work toward integration, not suppression. The goal is not to forget what happened but to function through what remains. God did not erase Moses' memory; He redefined its meaning.

Key Insight

The therapy of God is relational, not mechanical. He does not simply remove fear; He replaces it with awareness of Himself.

God's method with Moses was deeply personal. He did not offer explanations; He offered presence. Every divine "I will" dismantled a human "I can't." What Moses lost in confidence, he found in communion. The staff in his hand, once a tool of labor, became a symbol of divine partnership.

The same man who trembled before Pharaoh would later stand before God on Sinai—proof that transformation begins in encounter, not effort.

"So the Lord spoke to Moses face to face, as a man speaks to his friend."
— **Exodus 33:11 (NKJV)**

Fear may start the conversation, but presence always prevails.

Chapter 3 Reflection

Fear of the Unknown — Moses & the Call to Destiny

"Be strong and of good courage, do not fear nor be afraid of them; for the Lord your God, He is the One who goes with you. He will not leave you nor forsake you."
— *Deuteronomy 31:6 (NKJV)*

Awareness

What situation, transition, or calling in your life currently feels uncertain or intimidating? Where has fear of the unknown caused hesitation, delay, or retreat?

Insight

What did this chapter reveal about how fear of the unknown often disguises itself as logic, humility, or responsibility—particularly through questions like "Who am I?" or "What if it fails?"

Alignment

Which truth from Moses' encounter with God realigns your perspective—especially the truth that God's presence, not your preparedness, is the foundation for obedience?

Action

What specific step of obedience will you take this week despite uncertainty, trusting God to meet you in motion rather than waiting for complete clarity?

Declaration

"I am not governed by fear of the unknown. I move forward anchored in God's presence, not my limitations. The One who calls me goes with me, and I walk in courage, trust, and divine assurance."

CHAPTER 4

Fear of Insignificance and the Feeling of Irrelevance: Gideon & the Battle for Self-Worth

---

"The Lord is with you, mighty man of valor."
— *Judges 6:12 (NKJV)*

I grew up with a story that was both depressing and liberating. Depressing because of how it ended. Liberating because it opened my eyes to how parents, culture, and systems can quietly cage potential and alter the course of a person's life when truth is replaced by tradition.

She was the last born in her family, and one of the most brilliant students in our elementary school. Everyone knew she would go far. But her older sister struggled severely with learning difficulties. Their mother, determined to protect the older child's dignity, forced the younger one to repeat her class. "So your sister won't feel left behind," she said.

That decision—rooted in comparison and cultural expectation—became the beginning of her decline. The forced repetition broke something in her mind. It was a form of mental de-conditioning that soon spiraled into moral decline. The once-brilliant girl lost interest in school altogether. She began hanging around with older men, then married ones. Eventually, she became pregnant and dropped out.

People called her a home-wrecker. I didn't. I remembered the early signs—the spark fading, the conversations that changed, the confidence that disappeared. Birth order, family pressure, and misplaced priorities caged her destiny. As far as I know, she never recovered.

At the time, I didn't have the language to describe what I saw. But years later, while studying the life of Gideon, it all made sense.

"O my Lord, how can I save Israel? Indeed my clan is the weakest in Manasseh, and I am the least in my father's house." — **Judges 6:15 (NKJV)**

Every era has its battles, but few are as paralyzing as the war within. Before swords clash, before systems fail, and before nations fall, the greatest battles are fought in the mind—in the quiet chambers of self-perception, where identity either anchors faith or fuels fear.

Gideon's story is not merely about military conquest; it is the portrait of a man wrestling with invisibility. It is the story of a destiny trapped beneath self-doubt, a calling muted by comparison, and a potential crippled by the fear of insignificance.

The Context of Fear

A Society of Shrinking Souls

When we meet Gideon, Israel is living under Midianite oppression. For seven years, the people of God have known only defeat and deprivation. Their enemies ravage their crops, destroy their livelihood, and dictate their existence. Generational trauma has set in—not just materially but mentally. Israel, once bold under Joshua, has become a nation of hiding hearts.

The Midianite system did more than steal harvests; it rewired identity. People who once called themselves children of promise now call themselves survivors of defeat. They no longer think in terms of victory but in terms of preservation.

Fear has a way of shrinking vision until hiding feels safer than hoping.

By the time the Angel of the Lord visits Gideon, the nation's spirit is already broken. Their self-concept has been shaped by oppression. This is what I call **systemic smallness**—when circumstances sculpt how people see themselves, generation after generation, until they adapt to inferiority as normal.

Gideon, like many of us, was a product of that system.

Birth Order, Environment, and the Formation of Self-Perception

When Gideon says, "I am the least in my father's house," it is more than modesty—it is a diagnosis. He is describing his perceived position in his family's social and emotional hierarchy. In biblical culture, birth order determined worth, inheritance, and authority. To be the youngest was to be considered least significant, often expected to follow rather than lead.

In psychology, birth order theory suggests that early family roles influence lifelong patterns of behavior and self-concept. The firstborn often develops leadership instincts; the middle child learns negotiation; the youngest internalizes comparison. But in Gideon's case, the birth order wound deepened under national oppression—his personal insignificance was reinforced by collective hopelessness.

He was born into a family that was "the last in Manasseh," and then reminded daily that he was the last in that last family. That layered conditioning produced what I describe as **hierarchical inferiority**—a mindset that normalizes being overlooked.

When people are conditioned to think small, even divine encounters feel like exaggeration.

The Hidden Life

Fear in the Winepress

The introduction to Gideon in Judges 6:11 is striking:

"Gideon was threshing wheat in a winepress, in order to hide it from the Midianites."

Threshing wheat is meant to be done in open air, on a hill, where wind separates grain from chaff. But Gideon's fear drove him underground—literally. He was performing the right activity in the wrong place.

That image is profoundly symbolic. It captures what fear of insignificance does to potential: it buries productivity in secrecy, brilliance in timidity, purpose in fear.

He was not lazy—he was limited by his internal narrative. He had learned to succeed quietly, to avoid being seen, because being seen once meant being attacked.

Fear trains people to hide their greatness under the guise of humility.

And so, when God called Gideon "mighty man of valor," the words clashed violently with his inner reality. He had never been called "mighty" before—not by his family, not by his nation, not even by himself.

In that moment, divine truth met psychological conditioning. He was not just hiding wheat; he was hiding worth.

Bridge: What Gideon practiced outwardly—hiding, shrinking, staying unnoticed—was the behavioral expression of something deeper. Before the battle with Midian could ever be fought with swords, it had to be confronted in the mind.

The Internal Science of Low Self-Worth

Low self-worth is not only emotional—it is neurological. The brain encodes self-perception through repeated thoughts and experiences. Over time, negative self-talk becomes a cognitive default, hardwiring inferiority into the subconscious. Each time we repeat limiting thoughts like "I'm not enough" or "I'm the least," the brain strengthens those neural pathways, creating what neuroscience calls a negativity bias—a tendency to focus more on failure than success.

Spiritually, this is what Scripture calls a stronghold—an entrenched pattern of thought that resists truth. It is fear disguised as humility, reasoning disguised as realism. It manifests as self-sabotage, perfectionism, withdrawal, or chronic underachievement.

Low self-worth is not the absence of ability but the absence of accurate self-perception.

This is why people can be anointed but insecure, gifted but hesitant, called but conflicted. When self-perception does not align with divine definition, fear fills the gap. Gideon's fear was not of failure—it was of visibility. He feared what it meant to be seen, because being seen required responsibility.

The Divine Confrontation

Then the Lord appeared and said:

"The Lord is with you, mighty man of valor!" — **Judges 6:12 (NKJV)**

Notice: God's greeting was not a compliment; it was a correction. He spoke not to the man Gideon believed himself to be, but to the man heaven had ordained him to become. He bypassed Gideon's reality to announce his identity.

That single sentence contradicted years of internal programming. It was a divine interruption to everything Gideon had believed about himself.

Fear isolates identity; revelation restores it.

Bridge: Yet God did not stop at calling Gideon "mighty." He also exposed the mechanism that kept Gideon small. The battle wasn't only Midian outside—it was the inner voice that rehearsed limitation as truth.

The Art of Negative Self-Talk

When the Inner Critic Becomes a Spiritual Stronghold

"For as he thinks in his heart, so is he." — **Proverbs 23:7 (NKJV)**

Before Gideon ever fought the Midianites, he had to conquer an enemy within—his own thoughts. No sword, no shield, no battle plan could win this war because it was not fought in the valley of Jezreel, but in the corridors of the mind.

The most persistent voice of fear is not external; it's internal. It whispers through self-talk—those repetitive, invisible conversations that form the soundtrack of our self-perception. What the enemy cannot destroy through circumstance, he will attempt to distort through language.

The Psychology of Self-Talk

Psychologically, self-talk is the internal dialogue that influences mood, decision-making, and confidence. It can either affirm truth or reinforce fear. In neuroscience, each repeated thought strengthens a neural pathway, meaning that every word we internalize about ourselves becomes wiring in our brain. If the words are empowering, the brain builds a structure of courage. If they are negative, the mind constructs a fortress of fear.

Gideon's first recorded self-talk was defeatist:

"Indeed my clan is the weakest in Manasseh, and I am the least in my father's house." — **Judges 6:15 (NKJV)**

That single statement summarizes the essence of self-diminishment—a declaration that interprets calling through the lens of limitation. In modern clinical terms, this is cognitive distortion—the habit of filtering reality through negative assumptions until possibility feels impossible.

The danger is subtle but real: when negative self-talk goes unchallenged, it becomes identity talk. The brain stops analyzing those thoughts and begins to believe them as fact. Spiritually, this is how fear becomes a stronghold—not a passing feeling, but a fixed mindset that defies truth.

When self-talk contradicts divine truth, fear becomes theology.

The Anatomy of the Inner Critic

Every fearful person carries an inner critic—a voice that magnifies weakness and minimizes worth. For some, that critic sounds like a parent's disapproval. For others, it echoes failure, rejection, or unfulfilled expectations. Over time, this voice takes on spiritual authority, convincing the believer that humility means hiding, that wisdom means withdrawal, and that obedience must wait until they "feel ready."

But fear's vocabulary often sounds rational:

- "I'm not ready."
- "It's not the right time."
- "I don't have what it takes."

These statements seem harmless, but they carry spiritual weight because they form agreements—contracts in the soul that authorize limitation.

Fear doesn't always scream; sometimes it negotiates.

Every time we agree with those internal lies, we strengthen fear's dominion. And like Gideon, we end up threshing wheat in hidden places—productive but paralyzed, fruitful but fearful.

The Spiritual Dimension — Words as Gates

In the spiritual realm, words are gates. They open or close access to influence. Scripture says, *"Death and life are in the power of the tongue."* (Proverbs 18:21) This applies not only to what we say aloud but also to what we say within.

Gideon's transformation began when God interrupted his inner dialogue. He didn't first change Gideon's surroundings—He changed his speech pattern. God called him something he had never called himself: "Mighty man of valor." He introduced a new vocabulary to reprogram the mind of a man who had only ever known defeat.

The first step in breaking fear's stronghold is changing the language that sustains it.

When you begin to replace fear's narrative with faith's confession, you are not just speaking differently—you are building new neural pathways and opening spiritual portals to courage, creativity, and clarity. That is both the science and the spirit of renewal.

The Cycle of Low Self-Worth

Low self-worth follows a predictable cycle:

1. **Self-Comparison** — Measuring yourself by others' success.
2. **Negative Self-Talk** — Interpreting every experience through inadequacy.
3. **Emotional Withdrawal** — Avoiding opportunities to prevent rejection.

4. **Perceived Failure** — Mistaking fear-driven avoidance for proof of weakness.

5. **Reinforced Insecurity** — The mind says, "See? I told you I couldn't."

This is the same loop Gideon lived in until divine interruption. Each time he looked at his circumstances, fear reaffirmed his insignificance. But when he looked at the One speaking to him, truth redefined his worth.

Fear's cycle ends where revelation begins.

The Divine Intervention — God's Reprogramming Process

God's interaction with Gideon was not about building courage; it was about restoring identity. He didn't give him a strategy before giving him a name. He didn't outline the battle plan before rewriting the belief system.

"Go in this might of yours, and you shall save Israel from the hand of the Midianites. Have I not sent you?" — **Judges 6:14 (NKJV)**

That was not instruction—it was activation. God reminded him that he already had everything he needed; he just didn't believe it. He was not waiting for new strength; he was waiting for new self-perception.

This divine counseling moment mirrors what clinicians call cognitive restructuring—replacing distorted thoughts with truth until the brain forms a new reality. But God adds the supernatural dimension: presence. He doesn't just renew the mind; He revives the man.

Key Insight

Low self-worth is not humility; it is misplaced identity.

God never calls anyone "the least"—He calls them chosen, mighty, and sent.

Every divine assignment begins with redefinition. When you start calling yourself what God calls you, the inner critic loses jurisdiction. That is the secret of Gideon's transformation—not self-improvement, but divine identity recall.

Bridge: Once Gideon's inner language began to shift, God moved him to the next layer. Fear was not only personal; it had become structural—embedded in his home, normalized in his community, and reinforced through inherited altars.

When God Dismantles the Systems of Fear

Redefinition, Recalibration, and Release

"Go in this might of yours... Have I not sent you?" — **Judges 6:14 (NKJV)**

Every system sustained by fear—whether personal, familial, or cultural—requires divine interruption before it can be dismantled. God never delivers people from bondage without first confronting the internal structures that keep them bound. For Gideon, fear was not just an emotion; it was an ecosystem—a generational pattern of small thinking and self-diminishment that had shaped how his family and nation defined survival.

When the Lord appeared to Gideon, He was not only calling a man; He was confronting a system. The transformation that began in Gideon's mind would ripple through his household, his tribe, and ultimately his nation. What began as a conversation about identity became a campaign against idolatry—because idols are fear's monuments. They represent misplaced trust, human attempts to control what only God can command.

1. Redefinition — Identity Before Assignment

Before Gideon could fight Midian, God redefined his inner language. The phrase "Go in the strength you have" was not motivational—it was revelational. God was revealing that what Gideon already possessed internally was sufficient to initiate external change. Redefinition always precedes redirection.

Redefinition begins when God renames what fear mislabels.

Fear called Gideon "the least." God called him "mighty." Fear called his family "the weakest." God called them "chosen." The same pattern applies to us: fear names us by dysfunction, but God names us by design.

Clinically, this stage parallels the process of reframing in cognitive therapy—replacing distorted interpretations with accurate ones. Spiritually, it's repentance in its truest sense—not guilt-driven sorrow, but a change of perspective that produces transformation.

When Gideon accepted this new identity, his emotional posture began to shift. He was no longer speaking as the "least" but listening as one sent. This is the subtle but crucial point:

Fear begins with listening to yourself. Faith begins with listening to God.

2. Recalibration — Healing the Family System

Before Gideon could lead a nation, he had to cleanse his father's house. God's next instruction was deeply symbolic:

"Tear down the altar of Baal that your father has, and cut down the wooden image that is beside it." — **Judges 6:25 (NKJV)**

That altar represented more than idol worship—it symbolized inherited systems of fear and false dependency. His father's altar was a psychological mirror of generational trauma. Each stone was a memory, each pole a habit of misplaced faith.

Fear thrives in environments where false security is mistaken for stability.

Spiritually, Gideon's obedience dismantled generational idolatry. Psychologically, it was the breaking of an inherited mental model. Family systems theory teaches that each generation transmits patterns of belief and behavior unless someone interrupts the cycle. Gideon became that interruption.

He challenged the unspoken rule of his family system—"We don't confront what keeps us safe." That's what makes obedience in fearful environments so radical: it exposes what others have learned to accommodate. He tore down what his father built—not out of rebellion, but out of revelation.

Sometimes obedience feels like betrayal when fear has been normalized.

Through this act, Gideon recalibrated the spiritual and emotional atmosphere of his home. Every idol removed created room for divine presence. In counseling language, he was resetting his family's emotional thermostat; in spiritual terms, he was making room for glory.

3. Release — Courage as the Fruit of Alignment

Once Gideon's identity was redefined and his environment recalibrated, courage emerged naturally. It wasn't an emotion he forced; it was a byproduct of alignment. Fear dissipates when awareness of God becomes greater than awareness of self.

When the Spirit of the Lord came upon Gideon, Scripture says:

"Then he blew the trumpet, and the Abiezrites gathered behind him."
— Judges 6:34 (NKJV)

This was not the act of a fearful man. This was leadership born from healing. The same man who once hid now initiated a national movement. His transformation was not cosmetic; it was systemic.

Courage doesn't come from suppressing fear—it comes from surrendering control. Gideon didn't suddenly become fearless; he became faith-full. He still questioned, still sought confirmation, still laid out fleeces—but this time, he did so in the context of relationship, not retreat. There's a difference between doubt that seeks escape and doubt that seeks understanding. Gideon's doubt now lived within dialogue with God, not distance from Him.

Faith does not eliminate questions; it relocates them into conversation with God.

That is the essence of divine release—the movement from isolation to partnership, from reaction to revelation.

Fear operates in systems:

- Personally, as low self-worth.
- Familially, as generational dysfunction.
- Socially, as normalized mediocrity.

But when God intervenes, He doesn't treat symptoms—He restructures systems. He doesn't only deliver people from fear; He delivers them through fear by transforming how they see, think, and respond.

Gideon's story is a masterclass in divine psychology. It shows that courage is not the absence of trembling but the presence of truth. It teaches that self-esteem is not self-generated—it's identity reawakened through revelation. And it reveals that when God calls you, He's not asking you to prove your worth; He's inviting you to rediscover it in Him.

God does not recruit the qualified; He qualifies those willing to be redefined.

Fear is dismantled not by force but by formation—through identity, obedience, and intimacy.

Gideon's transformation wasn't instantaneous; it was sequential. First came redefinition—God spoke truth into his perception. Then came recalibration—he obeyed truth in his environment. Finally came release—he embodied truth before his generation.

This is how God still heals today: by confronting the system of fear one layer at a time until His presence replaces every false security.

Chapter 4 Reflection

Fear of Insignificance and the Feeling of Irrelevance — Gideon & the Battle for Self-Worth

---

"The Lord is with you, you mighty man of valor."
— *Judges 6:12 (NKJV)*

Awareness

In what moments do you feel most unseen, overlooked, or underestimated? Where has the inner critic shaped how you show up—or hide—despite potential and calling?

Insight

What did this chapter reveal about how fear of insignificance is formed through comparison, environment, family systems, or repeated self-talk? How has this fear disguised itself as humility, caution, or realism in your life?

Alignment

Which truth from Gideon's encounter with God corrects your self-perception—especially the truth that God names you by design, not by position, background, or past conditioning?

Action

What specific step will you take this week to come out of your "winepress"—to allow your gifts, voice, or leadership to be seen without apology or fear of comparison?

Declaration

"I am not defined by limitation, comparison, or invisibility. The Lord is with me, and I am who He says I am. I rise in the strength I have, clothed in divine identity, and I dismantle every altar of fear, smallness, and self-doubt."

CHAPTER 5

David's Curriculum in Overcoming Fear

"When I am afraid, I will trust in You."
Psalm 56:3 (NKJV)

Standing in Engedi — Where Fear Meets Faith

My travels once took me to Engedi, one of David's famous hideouts while he was running for his life. Standing by the springs and gazing at the caves carved into the rock triggered my imagination. No photograph could capture the haunting mix of beauty and danger in that place. Even today, my tour guide refused the idea of climbing into the caves: "Too risky," he said. "You never know what's inside—wild animals, serpents, or sudden collapse."

That was David's reality. The man after God's heart, anointed yet hunted. He lived much of his life in terrain that mirrored his internal world: unpredictable, dark, and filled with hidden threats.

Engedi made me realize that courage is not the absence of fear; it is the decision to trust in the middle of uncertainty.

Why This Chapter Matters

If you read no other chapter with reflection and meditation, pause here. This is a book within this book. David is, perhaps, the most transparent man in Scripture when it comes to fear. Others experienced it, but David recorded it: line by line, psalm by psalm, emotion by emotion. His life gives us a map of fear's many faces: spiritual, emotional, psychological, relational, and physical.

No other biblical figure reveals such an honest spectrum:

- Fear of rejection (His Parents)
- Fear of intimidation (Goliath)
- Fear of betrayal and workplace threat (Saul)
- Fear of loss and loneliness (exile)
- Fear of failure and divine judgment (Bathsheba episode)
- Fear of betrayal from within (Absalom's coup)
- Fear of death and legacy (his final psalms)

Each moment required a different spiritual prescription, yet one truth remained constant: David fought fear by running toward God, not away from Him.

Fear of Rejection – When My Father and Mother Forsake Me

"When my father and my mother forsake me, then the Lord will take care of me."
Psalm 27:10 (NKJV)

Before David ever faced the battlefield, he first faced the wound of being unseen. When the prophet Samuel came to anoint one of Jesse's sons, David was not even invited to the gathering. The prophet had to ask, "Are all your sons here?"—and only then did Jesse mention the youngest, who was tending the sheep (1 Samuel 16:11). That single omission carried a silent message: you are not significant enough to be considered.

One of the reasons people compromise their identity is rejection. Many destinies have been crippled by it. Yet David handled rejection differently. How he responded at home became the foundation for how he later confronted every other form of fear. The same David who declared, "The Lord is my light and my salvation—whom shall I fear?" had first learned to find light in the darkness of neglect. His courage did not begin on the battlefield—it began in the field of obscurity.

He refused to expose himself to the toxic atmosphere of comparison and resentment that could have corrupted his mind. Instead, he stayed at the back of the bush where he was wanted, even if it seemed irrelevant, because his peace was more valuable than proximity to those who couldn't perceive his worth. That decision preserved his mental and spiritual health.

David turned rejection into refinement. He found solace not in isolation but in solitude. He used the silence to develop skill, discipline, and devotion. He taught himself how to play music, learned how to shepherd with excellence, and became fluent in reflection. The wilderness became his classroom, and worship became his therapy.

The fear that causes many to compromise became for him the foundation of confidence. In solitude, he learned dependence on God, not validation from people. Each song he wrote was a step toward healing; each melody a declaration of resilience. By the time opportunity called, David's self-worth was no longer fragile, it was forged. What terrified others could not terrify him because he had already built an inner world fortified by divine approval.

How to Deal with Rejection and Build Courage Before the Battle of Destiny

David's journey offers a timeless pattern for those preparing for destiny after rejection:

- Protect Your Peace. Don't chase affirmation from places that continuously wound you. Choose solitude over toxicity; silence can heal what applause cannot.

- Redeem Your Solitude. Isolation becomes dangerous when it leads to bitterness, but it becomes holy when it births discovery. Use rejection as a workshop for reflection, creativity, and skill development.

- Anchor Identity in God, Not People. Rejection is only destructive when your identity depends on human validation. David's confidence came from the secret place where he heard, "The Lord is my Shepherd."

- Turn Pain into Preparation. Every painful experience can become training for the next level. Rejection prepared David to handle both the throne and the crowd without being defined by either.

- Build Inner Confidence Through Worship. Worship is the antidote to worthlessness. As David ministered to God alone, he discovered that divine presence is the cure for human absence.

By the time David stood before Goliath, he had already won the most personal battle—the battle for identity. His confidence was not borrowed from people's applause; it was built in private communion. His courage was not reactionary—it was rehearsed through daily dependence.

He learned early that true confidence is born in places where no one claps, and true courage is formed when no one notices.

Rejection, when surrendered to God, becomes the womb of resilience. It births confidence that no audience can inflate and no enemy can deflate

Fear on the Battlefield — Confronting Intimidation

His first public encounter with fear was collective. An entire army trembled under Goliath's taunts. David's courage did not spring from recklessness but from rehearsal. He had already faced lions and bears;

now he faced words and weapons. He overcame intimidation by remembering past faithfulness, reframing the threat, and declaring his covenant identity.

"The Lord who delivered me…" became his mental armor.

The Collapse of the Brave: What Happened to Saul's Army?

Fear does not discriminate by age, training or title. Saul's army consisted of professional warriors, men trained for combat, familiar with battle strategy, and equipped for defense. Yet, when Goliath appeared, these seasoned fighters fled.

What happened?

Their weapons remained sharp, but their confidence corroded. Their formation was intact, but their focus fractured. Their armor glittered in the sun, but their hearts trembled in the shadow of intimidation.

For forty days, Goliath's taunts echoed through the valley. Each repetition deepened their paralysis. The soldiers' bodies remembered the sound before their minds could resist it. Every morning they arose to the same sound, and every night they slept under the same intimidation. Fear became familiar, and familiarity numbed their fight. This is the psychology of intimidation: the enemy need not defeat you physically if he can defeat your will to respond. He only needs to manipulate your senses until perception replaces truth.

The Art and Science of Intimidation

Goliath understood psychological warfare. His size was spectacle; his voice was strategy. In the art of intimidation, the goal is dominance through sensory overload. When fear becomes loud, faith becomes faint. The target is the mind's confidence circuit. Once self-belief collapses, even the strongest arms lose strength. The weapon is repetition. Hearing the same threat repeatedly conditions the body to anticipate defeat.

Modern Goliaths still use this tactic through manipulation, power imbalance, or subtle control. The modern Goliath doesn't always carry a sword; sometimes he wields words, silence, or systems that reinforce inferiority.

Fear multiplies when the voice of the oppressor becomes louder than the conviction of purpose.

When David appeared, he came not as a warrior but as a courier. Courage often hides in the ordinary. Unlike Saul's soldiers, David's courage wasn't born in the barracks, it was forged in responsibility. He had been faithful in solitude, accountable for sheep no one else valued. When lions and bears came, he had no Plan B, no backup, no applause. His courage was born out of duty. Every scar was a classroom. Every deliverance was rehearsal for destiny.

Courage is not the absence of fear; it is the maturity of responsibility.

The Making of a Courageous Mind

The first time Scripture introduces David, he is absent. When Samuel arrived to anoint one of Jesse's sons, David wasn't even invited (1 Samuel 16:11). While others were being evaluated, he was elsewhere—unseen, unchosen, uncelebrated. Like Jephthah, David learned to navigate rejection early. He was the overlooked son who had to find validation in purpose, not position. His solitude taught him self-dialogue, a vital component of internal courage. But obscurity wasn't punishment; it was preparation. David learned to navigate rejection early. He carved solitude out of lonely places, and in that silence, he learned self-dialogue—a vital skill in conquering fear.. By the time he faced Goliath, he wasn't testing courage; he was expressing it.

Courage manifests in moments that leave no time for rehearsal. When David heard Goliath, he didn't pray for courage—he acted from conviction. The soldiers saw risk; David saw responsibility. They evaluated the enemy; David assessed the cause. "Is there not a cause?" he asked (1 Samuel 17:29).

Duty converted fear into fuel. Purpose silenced panic. When the sense of calling becomes greater than the fear of consequence, courage emerges naturally. Fear thrives in self-preservation, but courage lives in service.

The Spiritual Psychology of the Fight — Seeing Differently, Thinking Differently

"For we wrestle not against flesh and blood, but against principalities, against powers, against the rulers of the darkness of this world, against spiritual wickedness in high places."
Ephesians 6:12 (NKJV)

Every battle has a terrain—and in the story of David and Goliath, that terrain was not just physical but spiritual and psychological. The Valley of Elah became more than a battlefield; it was a proving ground of perception.

While Israel's army stood paralyzed, David stood poised. The same giant that crippled the soldiers and their commander in chief had no power over him. Why? Because David recognized what others could not: this was not a natural confrontation—it was a spiritual one.

The Terrain of Intimidation

From a human psychological standpoint, one strategy to overcome fear is exposure therapy gradual and repeated exposure to the fear trigger until desensitization occurs. Israel's army unknowingly practiced this for forty days as Goliath taunted them morning and evening. Yet, instead of becoming stronger, they grew weaker.

Why did exposure fail? Because this was not ordinary fear it was spiritually induced intimidation. The threat that paralyzed them did not arise from sight alone but from a demonic projection designed to infiltrate confidence and hijack identity.

Exposure to the spirit of fear does not bring healing; it deepens bondage. The more they heard Goliath, the smaller they saw themselves. The enemy's words became their meditation, and meditation became manifestation.

But David broke the pattern. He had already trained his mind in worship and his spirit in communion. The intimidation that echoed in others' minds found no landing place in his heart.

The Spirit–Mind–Body Connection

This encounter exposes the dynamic link between the spirit, the mind, and the body. Fear begins in the mind but is rooted in the spirit. Its symptoms manifest in the body—racing heart, trembling, paralysis—but its origin is spiritual.

David discerned this connection. He did not rely on human technique or self-confidence; he drew from spiritual discernment. He knew that the battle was not against flesh and blood but against unseen forces mocking the living God.

What Israel heard was not merely a man's roar—it was a demonic broadcast. The soldiers interpreted the threat through the natural lens of logic; David interpreted it through the spiritual lens of covenant.

Where others measured the problem, David measured the presence of God. Where others felt panic, he felt purpose. Where others sought strategy, he sought alignment.

It takes a spiritually discerning mind to know which weapon belongs to which realm. A psychological method cannot cure a spiritual affliction. Israel tried to fight a spiritual voice with human reasoning—and lost the inner battle before ever drawing a sword.

David: The Prototype of Spiritual Confrontation

David became the prototype of confronting fear on the level where it begins—the spiritual level. His courage was not adrenaline; it was alignment.

He fought fear with faith, worship, and awareness of covenant. He understood that the true fight begins within—long before it manifests without.

"The battle is the Lord's, and He will give you into our hands."
1 Samuel 17:47 (NKJV)

That statement was more than confidence—it was covenant consciousness. David's mind was not hypnotized by the size of Goliath; it was anchored in the size of his God.

Wisdom Highlight

Fear is a spirit before it becomes a feeling. When you confront it spiritually, its psychological and physical grip begins to lose power.

Not every fear is natural; some fears are spiritual projections.

Fear of Workplace Threat and Intimidation from Authority

"Fear is on every side; while they take counsel together against me, They scheme to take away my life."
Psalm 31:13 (NKJV)

David's victory over Goliath was not the end of his battle with fear—it was the beginning of another. After conquering the giant that held his nation hostage, David received what many would call a dream appointment: a position in the royal court, serving directly under the king he had just helped deliver. He became the president's personal aide, musician, and military leader—a promotion that looked prestigious on the outside but was perilous on the inside.

A Different Battlefield

The battlefield had shifted from the Valley of Elah to the palace halls of power. David's new enemy was not an uncircumcised Philistine but an anointed, unstable monarch. Saul, the commander-in-chief, was not a pagan adversary; he was a covenant man who had lost divine alignment but retained divine office.

David quickly learned that not all fears can be fought the same way. He could not fight Saul with the same boldness he used against Goliath, because the realm had changed. Saul was circumcised—he was under covenant. The spiritual strategy that gave David victory over Goliath would have been rebellion if used against Saul. Despite Saul's disobedience, David recognized his anointing and refused to overstep spiritual boundaries.

There are battles you do not fight with a sword; you win them through discernment.

The Psychology of Power and Fear

David's fear was real and relentless. His psalms expose the inner torment of living under daily threat:

"Deliver me from my enemies, O my God; defend me from those who rise up against me. Deliver me from the workers of iniquity, and save me from bloodthirsty men." — Psalm 59:1–2 (NKJV)

"They return at evening, they growl like a dog, and go all around the city." — Psalm 59:6 (NKJV)

He was afraid to go to work, yet he could not call in sick—doing so could have cost him his life. He lived in constant hyper-vigilance, a state that modern psychology would classify as chronic anxiety due to workplace trauma and power imbalance. Every sound, every glance, every royal command could be a potential death sentence.

But exposure to this fear could not cure it. You cannot desensitize yourself to a spirit of intimidation through repeated confrontation.

Some fears are not designed to be confronted—they must be outlasted through divine wisdom and spiritual endurance.

The Terrain of Treacherous Authority

The palace was a beautiful prison—a place of honor laced with hostility. David faced a form of fear few talk about: the fear of anointed authority. When the person threatening your safety also carries divine oil, the battle becomes treacherous.

He could not challenge Saul publicly without being branded rebellious; neither could he withdraw privately without being hunted. His fear was multidimensional—spiritual, emotional, psychological, and physical. Yet he refused to let fear dictate his response.

David's Strategy for Survival

David's response was not impulsive; it was strategic. He employed wisdom that bridged all realms—spiritual, psychological, and social:

- Wisdom — "He behaved himself wisely." David practiced emotional intelligence before the term existed. He understood that provoking Saul beyond measure would hasten his own death. He regulated his reactions, maintained decorum, and acted prudently in volatile situations. "David behaved himself wisely in all his ways; and the Lord was with him." — 1 Samuel 18:14

- Good Conduct — The Power of Character. His integrity became his defense. Even when falsely accused or misunderstood, David refused to give Saul legitimate grounds for destruction. Character restrained calamity.

- Strategic Alliances — The Ministry of Influence. David surrounded himself with allies who could speak to Saul—Jonathan, Michal, and Samuel. He understood the psychology of power and influence. Sometimes God delivers you through people who can access places you cannot.

- Prayer — The Weapon for Unfightable Battles. When human wisdom reached its limit, David turned to God in prayer. His psalms reveal that prayer was not his last resort; it was his life support.
  "Deliver me from my enemies, O Lord; teach me to do Your will." — Psalm 143:9–10

- Discernment — Knowing Which Weapon to Use. The greatest lesson David learned in Saul's court was that every fear has its realm, and every realm has its weapon.

You fight external threats with courage. You fight internal fear with faith. But you handle fearful authority with wisdom, restraint, and intercession.

There are people you cannot fight—only God can handle them. The wisdom of restraint is as powerful as the courage of confrontation.

Emotional Regulation and Spiritual Balance

David's psalms served as his therapy. They show a man processing trauma in real time—releasing fear through language and restoring faith through worship. In modern terms, he practiced emotional regulation through spiritual expression. Prayer stabilized his emotions; worship regulated his nervous system; reflection reframed his perspective.

He modeled what it means to live with emotional intelligence under divine pressure. Fear might visit, but it must not stay.

Fear from the Familiar — When Betrayal Wears a Familiar Face

"Even my own familiar friend in whom I trusted, Who ate my bread, has lifted up his heel against me."
Psalm 41:9 (NKJV)

Some battles break your body; others break your heart. David's final and fiercest encounter with fear came not from giants or kings—but from those he once loved and trusted. The betrayal of Absalom and Ahithophel introduced a deeper, more painful dimension of fear: the terror of realizing that the threat is no longer outside, but inside your circle.

The Anatomy of Familiar Fear

There is no strategy more paralyzing than treachery wrapped in trust. Absalom was David's son; Ahithophel was his counselor and confidant—his mentor in governance and strategy. Together, they formed a rebellion that struck David not only politically but psychologically.

This was not merely a coup; it was an emotional ambush. Fear from enemies can be faced; fear from friends must be survived. When someone who knows your weaknesses becomes your weapon-wielding adversary, every defense feels unsafe.

"For it is not an enemy who reproaches me; then I could bear it. Nor is it one who hates me... But it was you, a man my equal, My companion and my acquaintance." — Psalm 55:12–13 (NKJV)

David's words unveil the silent trauma of relational betrayal. The pain was not only in what they plotted—but in who was plotting.

The Psychology of Betrayal and Fear

Psychologically, betrayal generates a unique form of fear—anticipatory anxiety. The brain, conditioned to find safety in familiar faces, becomes confused when those faces turn hostile. The amygdala (the brain's alarm center) fires uncontrollably because trust and threat now share the same image.

David was traumatized by unpredictability. Every memory with Absalom carried double meaning—love intertwined with danger. His emotions and instincts were at war. How do you fight someone you once nursed? How do you defend yourself against someone who carries your features?

He could not conquer this fear with strategy; he could only survive it through surrender.

The Spiritual Dimension — When Love Must Not Lead

This was the realm where David's heart warred against his crown. He loved Absalom, yet Absalom had become the face of rebellion. David's decision to flee Jerusalem was not cowardice—it was discernment.

There are battles that love disqualifies you from fighting. He understood that if he stayed, he would have to destroy what he birthed. Leaving the city was not retreat—it was restraint.

Ahithophel's betrayal cut even deeper. Once the voice of trusted counsel, now the architect of treachery. Spiritually, Ahithophel represented the wounded wise—a man whose brilliance turned bitter because of unresolved offense (Many scholars trace his offense to Bathsheba's lineage. Scripture identifies Ahithophel of Giloh as the grandfather of Bathsheba: "Eliam the son of Ahithophel the Gilonite." — 2 Samuel 23:34; 2 Samuel 11:3 (NKJV).

Betrayal from the familiar carries a spirit of manipulation cloaked in reason. It hides behind history and uses proximity as leverage. David discerned that this was no longer about politics—it was a spiritual collision between covenantal destiny and relational loyalty.

David's Response — How to Survive Familiar Fear

- He Chose Flight Over Fight. David fled not because he was weak, but because he was wise. He refused to fight a battle that would destroy his seed and stain his soul. Some fears cannot be conquered—they must be outlasted in humility.

- He Redirected Pain Into Prayer. Instead of plotting vengeance, David turned to God.

  "O Lord, turn the counsel of Ahithophel into foolishness." — 2 Samuel 15:31 (NKJV) Prayer became the weapon that dismantled intellectual warfare.

- He Released the Outcome to Providence. On his way out of the city, David said,

  "If I find favor in the eyes of the Lord, He will bring me back." — 2 Samuel 15:25 (NKJV) This was not resignation—it was radical trust. Fear subsided because surrender replaced control.

- He Allowed God to Be the Judge. Absalom's rebellion ended without David drawing a sword. God settled what David submitted.

Some fears are not meant to be fought; they are meant to be entrusted. When the battle and fear come from the familiar, wisdom is not in winning—it is in not losing yourself.

The Emotional Aftermath

Even after Absalom's death, David's lament revealed the lasting emotional residue of familiar fear:

"O my son Absalom—my son, my son Absalom—if only I had died in your place!" — 2 Samuel 18:33 (NKJV)

Trauma often outlives the threat. The body may survive, but the heart needs time to recover. David grieved not just the loss of his son but the loss of innocence in trust.

Fear from the familiar is not easily forgotten—it reshapes how we love, lead, and lean on others.

Modern Parallels — Fear in Familiar Spaces

Many today experience similar wounds—fear of betrayal from those closest to them:

- A mentor turned manipulator.

- A friend turned competitor.

- A family member turned adversary.

This type of fear produces emotional fatigue, making it hard to trust again. But like David, you must remember: your healing is not in fighting back—it is in finding God's face again. Healing begins when you stop rehearsing the betrayal and start releasing the betrayer.

Betrayal from the familiar is the highest form of fear because it corrupts safety.

Fear in Exile — The Wilderness Season and the Psychology of Waiting

"When I am afraid, I will trust in You." — Psalm 56:3 (NKJV)
"My soul waits for the Lord more than those who watch for the morning." — Psalm 130:6 (NKJV)

Exile is not always a place of punishment; sometimes, it is the classroom of preparation. After escaping Saul's threats and surviving betrayal from those closest to him, David entered the most silent yet shaping chapter of his life—the wilderness. The noise of battle was gone, but a new enemy emerged: the fear of waiting.

The wilderness was not filled with roaring giants or spears—it was filled with questions. When will this end? Has God forgotten me? Will His promise still come to pass?

This was fear stripped of noise—the kind that whispers in silence and feeds on uncertainty.

The Psychology of Waiting

Waiting tests the mind in ways warfare never does. In battle, adrenaline provides clarity and focus. In waiting, the absence of motion amplifies anxiety. The human brain, wired for prediction and control, struggles when it cannot calculate outcomes.

David's wilderness lasted years—years of displacement, deprivation, and deferred destiny. He had the promise of kingship but none of its privileges. From a psychological perspective, he was living with cognitive dissonance—knowing what God said, yet seeing nothing that resembled it.

Spiritually, it was an advanced course in trust. Emotionally, it was an ongoing exposure to uncertainty. Physically, it was survival.

Fear of Delay and the Crisis of Timing

Fear in exile often manifests as fear of delay. When divine timing seems slow, the mind begins to interpret silence as rejection. David wrestled with this:

"How long, O Lord? Will You forget me forever? How long will You hide Your face from me?" — Psalm 13:1 (NKJV)

The gap between anointing and appointing was David's greatest test. He had the oil, but not the opportunity. He had prophecy, but no platform.

This tension produces a psychological fatigue many believers know well—the exhaustion of waiting without visible progress.

But God was not absent; He was conditioning. Waiting was not punishment—it was preparation for governance. The wilderness was God's laboratory for emotional mastery, spiritual discernment, and leadership formation.

The Spiritual Function of Silence

God's silence was not indifference—it was instruction. When God hides His voice, He's not abandoning you; He's training your perception. David learned to locate God in stillness, not spectacle.

"Be still, and know that I am God." — Psalm 46:10 (NKJV)

Stillness became David's spiritual strategy. He realized that faith must grow muscles in the dark before it shines in daylight. This was where his psalms of trust were birthed—not from a throne, but from caves.

The Wilderness as Therapy

From a psychological perspective, the wilderness functioned as trauma recalibration. After years of living under threat, David's nervous system needed regulation. The caves of Adullam became his recovery clinic—a place to decompress from chronic hyper-vigilance and rebuild emotional rhythm.

He gathered men who were distressed, indebted, and discontented (1 Samuel 22:2)—people whose emotional states mirrored his own. In ministering to them, David unknowingly ministered to himself. Service became his therapy.

Helping others through their fear becomes one of the ways God heals yours.

The Fear of the Unknown

In exile, David faced a subtler kind of fear—the fear of what's next. There were no maps, no timelines, no assurances. Fear of the unknown often tempts the heart toward self-made shortcuts. Saul's impatience once cost him his kingdom; David learned to resist that same urge.

He discovered that waiting is warfare. Every delay demands discernment—will you interpret it as God's absence or as God's architecture?

"Wait on the Lord; be of good courage, and He shall strengthen your heart." — Psalm 27:14 (NKJV)

Faith in waiting is not passive; it is persistent courage sustained by memory.

The Discipline of Remembering

David conquered the fear of waiting through spiritual remembrance. He rehearsed God's past faithfulness to stabilize present fear. Memory became the antidote to anxiety.

When he wrote,
"I sought the Lord, and He heard me, and delivered me from all my fears." — Psalm 34:4 (NKJV)
he was testifying that deliverance began in memory before it manifested in motion.

Reflection restores reality. By recalling God's prior interventions, David reprogrammed his emotions from panic to peace.

When fear thrives in delay, worship becomes the weapon that keeps you anchored. The wilderness is not a wasteland—it is where faith grows roots deep enough to outlast drought.

The Transformation of Fear

By the end of his exile, David was no longer the shepherd boy who fought lions in the field or the warrior who faced giants in the valley. The wilderness transformed him into a king fit for destiny.

He had faced fear in every realm—spiritual, institutional, relational, and existential—and each taught him a new language of courage.

He learned to fight fear spiritually through worship and covenant. He managed fear psychologically through wisdom and restraint. He survived fear relationally through prayer and surrender.

He transcended fear existentially through trust and waiting.

When he finally sat on the throne, his confidence was not built on charisma but on character formed in caves.

Fear in waiting is defeated by the memory of God's faithfulness.

Fear of Failure and Divine Judgment — When Grace Meets the Limits of Man

"Do not cast me away from Your presence, And do not take Your Holy Spirit from me."
Psalm 51:11 (NKJV)

I am yet to meet a man who has not wrestled with the fear of failure. Among all the shades of fear, this may be the most crippling. It begins subtly—with worry, anxiety, and the quiet whisper of inadequacy. It often feeds on imagination, projecting disasters that never happen. Yet even when the fear itself is unfounded, it robs us of our most irreplaceable asset—time.

But when the failure you once feared actually happens, it pierces deeper than imagination—it becomes identity. That is where David found himself after the Bathsheba episode. His fear of failure was not anticipatory—it was realized. It was the moment when private weakness became public exposure, when the man after God's heart crossed a line he could not justify.

This was no ordinary fear; it was the terror of divine separation. David had faced enemies, rejection, and betrayal, but this time, the enemy was within. It was not the fear of man—it was the fear of himself. His moral failure revealed a dimension of darkness he did not know existed. He had wielded authority well on the battlefield, but here he abused it in the bedroom. The sin was not only in the act—it was in the misuse of power and the blindness of privilege.

David's psalms from that season are the cries of a man who no longer feared death, but disconnection.

74

"Against You, You only, have I sinned, and done this evil in Your sight." — Psalm 51:4 (NKJV)

The fear of judgment was not about punishment—it was about presence. He could live without the crown, but not without the Spirit. For David, the ultimate horror was annihilation from divine fellowship. His words, "Do not take Your Holy Spirit from me," echo the trauma of watching Saul lose his anointing.

In this moment, fear did not drive him to flight or fight—it drove him to brokenness. It was in failure that David learned that the only antidote to judgment is mercy, and mercy is at the discretion of God.

David's repentance was not an argument for leniency—it was a cry for restoration. He had seen what divine rejection looked like and could not survive another version of it. His psalm became a mirror for every soul that has failed deeply yet longs desperately for redemption.

Understanding the Psychology of Failure and Judgment

Fear of failure begins as anxiety about outcomes, but matures into despair when identity is attached to performance.

Like Job, fear itself can attract what we dread. Job confessed, "The thing I greatly feared has come upon me." (Job 3:25). His fear cooperated with affliction. Likewise, David's moral collapse revealed how unchecked tendencies within can partner with the adversary without.

Failure exposes the fragility of self-righteousness. Until failure humbles us, we assume our moral strength is our security.

Fear of divine judgment refines love. When love matures, it replaces fear—not because judgment ceases to exist, but because mercy rewrites the verdict.

Lessons from David's Darkest Season

- Face Failure Without Denial. True repentance begins where excuses end. David did not minimize his sin; he magnified God's mercy.

- Accept Consequences Without Condemnation. Mercy doesn't always cancel consequences, but it restores relationship.

- Learn to Fear Losing Presence More Than Losing Position. David's restoration was not the return of status—it was the return of intimacy.

- Let Brokenness Birth Wisdom. Psalm 51 is not the cry of a fallen man; it is the curriculum of recovery. Out of that failure came a new dimension of compassion, humility, and discernment.

- Replace Self-Reliance with Grace-Dependence. The fear of failure fades where grace is understood. Failure ends where dependence begins.

Chapter 5 Reflection

"When I am afraid, I will trust in You."
— *Psalm 56:3 (NKJV)*

Awareness

What situation in your life currently feels like Engedi—a place where danger, uncertainty, or tension surrounds you? Where has fear been shaping your thoughts, emotions, or physical responses?

Insight

What did this chapter reveal about the different faces of fear David encountered—intimidation, authority, betrayal, waiting—and the wisdom required to respond differently in each season?

Alignment

Which truth from David's life realigns your perspective—especially the truth that fear does not disqualify faith, and that trust is a decision made in the presence of threat, not the absence of it?

Action

What intentional practice will you engage this week—worship, prayer, reflection, or remembrance of past deliverance—to quiet fear and strengthen trust in God's presence?

Declaration

"When I am afraid, I will trust in the Lord. Fear does not govern my decisions or define my future. God is my refuge, my confidence, and my covenant-keeper. I walk forward in courage, anchored in His faithfulness."

CHAPTER 6

The Battle Within: Elijah's Fear and Depression

The character we want to understudy and through him, uncover the subtlety and severity of fear's attack is the type we often perceive as fearless, bold, and unshakable. These are the ones who seem capable of facing any challenge and conquering every circumstance. To the onlooker, they appear invincible. People rarely imagine the possibility of their inner battles until their private pain, struggles, and fears surface in public.

This chapter is for the strong ones who fight alone. For those whose titles, roles, or reputation have become armor that hides the tremor of fear within. It is for the men and women who stand tall in public yet collapse in private. For those we have immortalized in strength and denied permission to feel. In many cultures, especially among men, showing fear is treated as weakness, and vulnerability is equated with failure. Yet fear is an equal opportunity afflicter. It respects no title, gender, or anointing. It visits prophets and kings, parents and pastors, CEOs and intercessors alike.

If you have ever been expected to have all the answers while wrestling with questions of your own, or if you have ever been the one others run to while secretly wishing someone would notice your exhaustion, this chapter is written with you in mind. Elijah's story unveils a side of fear that creeps into the hearts of the powerful not through sin or failure but through fatigue, isolation, and the unspoken pressure to remain invincible.

God is familiar with human frailty. He meets us not only at the altar of fire but also in the cave of fear. His whisper still reaches those who have lost their voice beneath the weight of unspoken battles.

Elijah's Entrance: Strength Before the Storm

The first time Elijah appeared in the pages of history, nothing about him suggested a struggle with rejection, abandonment, or identity. Purpose was never his issue. His background was never mentioned, yet his presence radiated strength and confidence. He did not fit the profile of a man weighed down by insecurity or disadvantaged beginnings.

His entrance was both dramatic and commanding:

"And Elijah the Tishbite, of the inhabitants of Gilead, said to Ahab, 'As the Lord God of Israel lives, before whom I stand, there shall not be dew nor rain these years except at my word.'" — 1 Kings 17:1 (NKJV)

Elijah emerged on the national scene with undeniable spiritual authority and unshakable conviction. His words carried the full weight of heaven's government. Without hesitation or fear, he confronted the most powerful man in his nation and declared divine judgment with absolute certainty.

If we did not know how his story ended, it would be almost impossible to imagine that this same prophet who commanded the heavens with a word would one day be crippled by fear.

To understand how fear found its way into Elijah's heart, we must first see the man he was before the storm. His story began not with weakness but with strength. He stepped out of obscurity with a voice that silenced kings and shifted climates. There was no trace of hesitation, no evidence of insecurity, and no sign of self-doubt. His words carried fire, and his presence drew reverence.

At first glance, Elijah seemed the least likely candidate for fear. He had no recorded lineage, yet he spoke with the confidence of one who knew exactly where he stood: before the Lord God of Israel. That awareness of divine presence was the source of his courage. Every act of boldness flowed from the consciousness of standing before God. Yet even such proximity to the divine does not erase human vulnerability. The same man who once stood before kings would later flee from a single voice.

Here begins the paradox of power. Strength without rest becomes fragile. Confidence without renewal becomes unstable. Even the fearless can quietly become afraid.

Elijah, like many of us, started with a full cup. His zeal, focus, and conviction overflowed with divine energy and purpose. But as you read, pause and reflect. Can you relate to his mindset or psychology? He was a doer, a leader of excellence, a man who took charge and executed divine assignments without hesitation. Perhaps you too have been that person—the one who must always be strong for others, the one who carries expectations that leave little room for weakness. In Elijah, we see not only the prophet but also the human being behind the mantle.

The Pressure of Power and Public Expectation

Every position of responsibility carries weight. The same grace, skill, or competence that empowers a person to lead also exposes them to pressures that others rarely see. Elijah lived under this tension. His words shaped national direction, and his actions carried divine consequence. Yet behind every public victory was a private burden that few could imagine.

Public assignment is a sacred trust, but it is also a heavy calling. Those who carry visible or high-stakes responsibilities live with constant pressure to deliver, to stay composed under scrutiny, and to appear strong even when they are weary. Their lives become symbols of confidence and control. For Elijah, that meant being the visible expression of God's authority in a season of national rebellion. For many today, it means being the anchor in spaces that depend on your stability.

You do not have to stand on a mountain to feel what Elijah felt. The physician who must keep calm when a patient's life hangs in the balance. The parent who swallows fear to comfort a child. The business owner who hides financial stress to protect their staff. The teacher who holds a classroom together while quietly breaking inside. The leader who cannot show uncertainty because others depend on their composure. These are the modern Elijahs.

The expectation to remain strong often silences the need for help. The world rarely gives permission to tremble. Many therefore learn to suppress fear, grief, or frustration to preserve an image of control. Over time, this restraint becomes exhausting. The inner life begins to suffocate under the weight of responsibility. The heart grows weary from pretending to be unbreakable.

Elijah's experience reflects this human tension. His assignment required confrontation, courage, and consistency, but it also demanded solitude and secrecy. The longer he carried responsibility without replenishment, the more isolated he became. When people give constantly without receiving, depletion becomes inevitable. Even the strongest eventually reach their limit.

The Mount Carmel experience, though glorious, revealed the first signs of strain. On that mountain, Elijah faced opposition, spiritual warfare, and the expectations of an entire nation. He poured out everything—emotionally, physically, and spiritually. The fire that fell from heaven marked victory, yet it also marked exhaustion. After that moment, Elijah kept moving without rest or reflection. He went from intense action to another demand without time to recover.

This is how breakdown begins. Fear does not always arrive suddenly. It grows quietly in the shadows of fatigue and imbalance.

Jezebel's threat did not create Elijah's fear; it simply exposed what weariness had already planted.

The lesson is clear. Responsibility, visibility, and influence require intentional renewal. Strength that is not replenished becomes fragile. Passion that is not balanced with rest becomes destructive. Every demanding role needs private restoration. Without it, even the strongest eventually bend under the weight of unspoken expectations.

As you read this, pause and ask yourself: Where are you giving more than you are receiving? What areas of your life demand constant strength, composure, or control? Are you pouring from a full cup or surviving on empty? Every provider, parent, leader, and professional knows the pressure of appearing unshaken when the heart is weary. The truth is that constant performance without renewal breeds quiet depletion.

Like Elijah, many of us have learned to keep functioning long after the warning signs appear. We show up for others, manage crises, and keep moving because stopping feels like failure. Yet the human soul was never designed for endless output. Rest is not a sign of weakness but a form of wisdom. Renewal is not a luxury; it is a necessity for endurance.

Before fear ever takes hold, fatigue usually whispers first. It speaks through sleepless nights, short tempers, emotional numbness, or loss of joy. Those moments are invitations to pause, to replenish, and to reconnect with the Source of strength. The most courageous act is not always pressing forward; sometimes it is learning when to rest.

The Breaking Point

Every person has a threshold, a point where emotional, mental, or spiritual strain becomes too heavy to bear. For Elijah, that moment came not in battle but in silence. After his public triumph on Mount Carmel, he received a single message from Queen Jezebel, promising to take his life. On the surface, it was a threat, but beneath it lay something deeper. Jezebel's words touched a wound that fatigue had already opened.

Elijah, the same man who once commanded fire from heaven, now ran for his life. The contrast is striking. The prophet who had stood before kings was now hiding from a woman's threat. Yet this was not about cowardice. It was about collapse. Exhaustion had drained the emotional and spiritual reserves that once sustained him. When strength runs low, even small threats can feel overwhelming.

The human mind interprets danger differently when tired. Fatigue magnifies fear. Perspective narrows. Hope fades. For Elijah, Jezebel's message was not simply a warning; it became the voice of every unhealed emotion he had suppressed—loneliness, frustration, disappointment, and isolation. The weight of years of confrontation now pressed against a weary heart.

He fled into the wilderness and prayed that his life would end. This was not rebellion; it was surrender to exhaustion. Elijah's words in that moment reveal the language of burnout: "It is enough. Take my life." When people say they have had enough, they are not always rejecting their purpose; they are often expressing depletion. They have reached the limit of what their soul can carry.

In many ways, Elijah's breaking point mirrors our own. The healthcare provider who silently absorbs others' pain until it becomes their own. The parent who holds everything together but cries behind closed doors. The leader who motivates others but no longer believes their own words. The business owner who carries responsibility for many but feels unseen. These are modern echoes of Elijah's cry.

Jezebel did not create Elijah's fear; she exposed his fatigue. Her threat simply illuminated what long-term strain had already eroded. The prophet's reaction teaches us that fear is often the symptom, not the cause. Beneath it lies emotional depletion, loneliness, and the human need for rest.

Even in his lowest moment, God did not condemn Elijah. Instead, He initiated recovery. That moment marks a turning point in how God deals with human weakness—not through rebuke, but through restoration.

The Anatomy of Fear – When Strength Becomes a Snare

Fear rarely begins in a single moment; it evolves through a process. In Elijah's case, Jezebel's threat was not the true cause of his fear. It was the trigger that exposed internal weaknesses that had long gone unaddressed. His fear was a culmination of emotional fatigue, spiritual imbalance, and psychological isolation.

Unlike David, whose psalms revealed a rhythm of emotional release through prayer, worship, and self-reflection, Elijah lived with no visible outlet for his inner world. We saw his public victories but not his private processing. His life was marked by confrontation and performance, not introspection. While David fought both on the battlefield and in his soul, Elijah fought almost exclusively in public. The absence of consistent personal communion beyond prophetic encounters left him spiritually charged but emotionally drained.

Jezebel's words, though external, collided with an internal void. Elijah had carried authority for so long that he began to mistake divine partnership for personal power. His statement, "There shall not be dew nor rain except at my word," revealed confidence, but over time that confidence drifted toward self-reliance. The strength that once came from standing before God began to transform into an identity anchored in performance.

Fear often thrives in such imbalance. When one's sense of worth or strength becomes tied to output or recognition, any threat to control feels existential. Elijah's exaggerated sense of self had become both his armor and his Achilles heel. What began as divine confidence slowly mutated into overconfidence. He believed he was the only righteous one left, and in doing so, he isolated himself emotionally and spiritually. God later corrected this illusion by reminding him that seven thousand others had not bowed to Baal.

This illusion of exclusivity deepened Elijah's despair. The moment Jezebel threatened him, the prophet who once stood as heaven's voice felt completely alone and powerless. Depression entered quietly through exhaustion, and hopelessness followed. His words, "It is enough, take my life," revealed not rebellion but collapse. What had once been holy boldness now turned into internal chaos.

Elijah's condition mirrors the emotional trajectory of many who carry great responsibility. Continuous exposure to high stakes, without avenues for rest or reflection, creates a vacuum where fear grows unchecked. The absence of healthy emotional expression can turn courage into control, and faith into frustration. Overconfidence, just like low self-esteem, can destroy a person from within.

God, in His mercy, did not reject Elijah but also did not overlook his folly. Divine compassion met human frailty, yet there were consequences. Elijah's appointment was concluded, and Elisha was anointed in his place. God restored him but restructured his assignment. Fear had revealed what pride had hidden—the limits of human strength without continual renewal.

This is the sobering truth about fear. It does not always attack the weak. Sometimes it hunts the strong, the accomplished, and the overconfident. Elijah's story shows that unchecked success without self-awareness can lead to silent collapse. When a person stops cultivating humility, reflection, and rest, even divine victories can become emotional traps.

Elijah's story invites us to look beyond surface definitions of fear. Sometimes the source of fear is not weakness but pride. It is the quiet belief that we must never fail, that our worth depends on constant victory. This mindset creates an illusion of control that leaves no room for human frailty. The same drive that fuels excellence can, without balance, become the soil of anxiety.

Many live with what can be called the "I would rather die than fail" syndrome. It sounds noble, but it is often rooted in perfectionism and the fear of imperfection. The inability to accept limitation or loss breeds torment, not peace. Elijah had carried such intensity for so long that failure became unthinkable. When defeat seemed possible, he broke under the weight of it. Jezebel was not a typical adversary; she was strategic, manipulative, and psychologically threatening. She did not confront Elijah on the mountain. She reached for his mind. The moment he realized that the battle had shifted from external to internal, despair became inevitable. His request for death was not only exhaustion; it was the collapse of identity built on success.

This is where fear reveals its most deceptive form. It hides beneath the surface of competence, ambition, and high performance. It wears the mask of confidence but feeds on the terror of inadequacy. Healing begins when we acknowledge that true strength is not in never failing but in remaining humble enough to recover, reflect, and realign.

The Divine Therapy – When God Meets You in Retreat

Every encounter with God's healing begins with human decision. Before God stepped in, Elijah took a step away. He chose to change location. He left his servant in Beersheba and journeyed alone into the wilderness. That decision marked the beginning of his personal retreat, a space where he could process pain, exhaustion, and disappointment away from public demand.

In the wilderness, Elijah did not pray for victory. He prayed for death. That prayer revealed a man whose courage had turned to collapse. He was not faithless, but he was finished. The emotional toll of ministry, isolation, and disappointment had drained his will to continue. Yet even in that broken moment, his retreat positioned him for restoration. Sometimes stepping away is not escape; it is the first step toward healing.

As he slept under the tree, God began the work Elijah could not begin for himself. Heaven entered his exhaustion. An angel touched him and said, "Arise and eat." Divine therapy often starts where human effort ends. God did not begin with correction but with care. He addressed the physical before addressing the spiritual. The meal was not symbolic; it was essential. Elijah needed strength before revelation.

After eating and resting, Elijah continued deeper into solitude. Strengthened by that food, he fasted and traveled forty days to Mount Horeb, the mountain of God. This was no ordinary journey. It was a forty day retreat of silence, reflection, and confrontation with his inner life. God allowed the process to unfold before speaking. True transformation takes time, and solitude exposes what noise conceals.

When Elijah finally reached Horeb, God asked, "What are you doing here, Elijah?" The question was not for information but for introspection. It was an invitation to self-awareness. Twice Elijah gave the same answer, revealing how deeply entrenched his mindset had become: "I have been very zealous... I alone am left." This was not humility speaking but pride disguised as loneliness. Elijah had placed himself at the center of God's plan, and his exhaustion revealed the cost of that illusion.

Then came the divine correction wrapped in gentleness. God revealed Himself, not through wind, earthquake, or fire, but through a still small voice. The same God who once sent fire now whispered peace. Elijah had to learn that God's presence is not always loud or dramatic. The stillness was God's therapy for a restless soul.

Only after Elijah had listened did God restore his mission. The prophet was recommissioned to anoint Hazael, Jehu, and Elisha. Yet the order of revelation is significant. Elijah was replaced before he was reassured. God first appointed Elisha as his successor, then revealed that seven thousand others remained faithful. Divine therapy involves truth before comfort. God loved Elijah enough to free him from the illusion that he was indispensable.

There is another insight hidden within this moment. God never verbally told Elijah that he was carrying more than he was designed to handle. There is no record of God saying, "You are doing too much." Yet the succession plan itself spoke loudly. Replacing Elijah with three different people was a silent but unmistakable message. Elijah was doing work that required three assignments, three capacities, and three graces. He had become a one man army, operating beyond the limits of human endurance.

Many of us fall into the same pattern. We become territorial in service. We believe no one can do it like us. We take on what belongs to a team because we equate productivity with purpose and exhaustion with obedience. Overwork becomes a badge of honor rather than a warning sign. Yet imbalance carries fear with it, fear of underperformance, fear of losing control, fear of not being enough. Elijah's story reminds us that even in spiritual work, overload often reveals a misplaced identity.

This encounter teaches that recovery requires participation. Elijah took the first step by retreating, resting, and making space for God to intervene. Healing followed alignment. God responded not because Elijah was perfect, but because he was honest enough to stop running and start resting.

The divine pattern is consistent even today. When strength fades, God invites us into retreat. Rest, nourishment, reflection, and correction all form part of His restoration plan. He meets us where our endurance ends and begins the quiet work of renewal.

Lessons from Elijah's Fear

Elijah's story stands as both a warning and a guide. His journey reveals that fear is not always the result of weakness; sometimes it is the product of success unbalanced by self-awareness. What we call collapse often begins long before it becomes visible. Beneath Elijah's exhaustion lay a complex mix of pride, overconfidence, isolation, and unrealistic expectations of himself.

The first lesson is that fear often disguises itself. It hides behind busyness, confidence, and performance. The person who appears most in control may be the one quietly holding back panic. Fear feeds on imbalance. It grows when we measure our worth by output, when we serve without renewal, and when we mistake control for competence.

The second lesson is that exhaustion creates distortion. Fatigue narrows vision and amplifies emotions. What appears catastrophic in weariness may look manageable in rest. God understood this when He restored Elijah's body before addressing his beliefs. Physical renewal is not separate from spiritual health. Many who think they need deliverance actually need rest.

The third lesson is that self-righteousness is a silent destroyer. Elijah's declaration, "I alone am left," revealed not only loneliness but an inflated sense of importance. Pride and fear are two sides of the same coin—one overestimates self, the other underestimates grace. When we begin to see ourselves as irreplaceable, we carry burdens we were never designed to bear.

The fourth lesson is that true strength is found in humility. Elijah rediscovered God not in thunder or fire but in a still small voice. Real courage does not always roar; sometimes it whispers. Power that flows from peace endures longer than power that flows from pressure.

The fifth lesson is that isolation magnifies fear. Elijah withdrew into solitude, convinced he was alone, but his separation distorted reality. Connection is a safeguard against despair. God reminded him that seven thousand others remained faithful. The revelation of community helped dismantle the illusion of aloneness. In the same way, healing begins when we let others see our humanity.

The final lesson is that God restores even after failure. Elijah's journey ended with grace, not disgrace. Though his appointment concluded, his purpose did not die with it. He became a mentor to Elisha, passing on his wisdom and experience. God did not discard him; He redirected him. Restoration is never punishment—it is preparation for new alignment.

Elijah's story teaches us that fear is multi-dimensional. It can emerge from exhaustion, pride, or pressure, but in every form, it is conquerable through humility, rest, truth, and divine perspective. The same God who met Elijah under the juniper tree still meets us in our weariness. His therapy remains the same: rest, revelation, and renewal.

Chapter 6 Reflection

"And after the fire a still small voice."
— *1 Kings 19:12 (NKJV)*

Awareness

Where in your life have you been running on empty while still pushing forward? What responsibilities, expectations, or roles have required constant strength while quietly draining your reserves?

Insight

What did this chapter reveal about how fear can emerge not from weakness, but from exhaustion, overextension, pride, or self-reliance? How has doing too much—or believing you must do it alone—contributed to emotional or spiritual depletion?

Alignment

Which truth from Elijah's encounter with God realigns your perspective—especially the truth that rest is not failure, withdrawal is not disobedience, and God's presence often restores us through stillness rather than intensity?

Action

What intentional step will you take this week to enter a posture of retreat—rest, silence, delegation, nourishment, or prayer—allowing God to restore what striving has depleted?

Declaration

"I release the pressure to be everything to everyone. I am sustained by grace, not by constant effort. I embrace rest as sacred, not selfish.

God meets me in stillness, and I am being renewed in body, soul, and spirit."

CHAPTER 7

Beyond Fear

The Power of Purpose in Esther

"Purpose is the antidote to fear. It gives pain meaning and transforms risk into obedience."

Dr. Joke Solanke

The Silent Face of Fear

Every generation has its Esthers—women who appear composed, competent, and crowned with favor, yet live under invisible fear. Esther's fear was not expressed through panic or trembling; it was buried beneath obedience and strategy. She learned to survive in a system that demanded silence, restraint, and calculated appearances.

Unlike Elijah, whose fear erupted in exhaustion, Esther's fear was subtle and social. Her life was governed by rules that made emotion a liability. To approach her own husband without invitation meant death. To speak without permission risked disgrace. To reveal her true identity could mean extermination. She lived in a palace of privilege that doubled as a cage of control.

Esther's story opens a different window into fear—one shaped not by threat of war but by the fear of exposure and rejection. It is the fear that visits those who must be perfect to be accepted, silent to stay safe, and compliant to survive. Her courage did not begin in confidence; it began in constraint.

Many today live in that same tension. They navigate professional spaces, marriages, and ministries where silence feels safer than honesty. They hide emotion to keep peace and suppress identity to keep position. Esther's story speaks to them—the ones whose strength is misunderstood as comfort, whose obedience masks anxiety, and whose fear is disciplined, not displayed.

Fear Redefined

When You Have Nothing Left to Lose

There is a unique kind of fear that loses its power once a person has lost almost everything. When life has stripped away comfort, certainty, and the illusion of safety, fear begins to change shape. For Esther, fear was not a sudden emotion but a lifelong companion. She learned to live beside it, to function through it, and eventually, to master it.

Her story begins with loss. It is not recorded what caused the death of her parents, but historical and cultural evidence suggest that she was a war orphan—one of many displaced during Persia's expansion. If so, her earliest memories were shaped by chaos, uncertainty, and survival in a foreign land. The child who once feared everything eventually became the woman who feared nothing because there was nothing left to lose.

Her nearest relative, Mordecai, took her in and raised her. Scripture describes him as a man stationed at the king's gate, a position of security and surveillance in the government palace. He was dutiful, loyal, and disciplined—a man of structure rather than sentiment. Esther did not grow up in an environment of emotional softness or maternal comfort. The love of a guardian is not the same as the love of a parent. She had to mature quickly, adapt silently, and learn courage through endurance.

Perhaps that is why fear never fully ruled her—it had been her teacher. Her courage was not the absence of fear but the mastery of it. She did not panic when life shifted because she had already known instability. She did not tremble before the king because she had already faced greater losses. Pain had become her preparation.

It is possible that fear thrives most in comfort. Those who have never been stretched or stripped are often more vulnerable to fear's influence because comfort teaches dependency on predictability. Esther's world offered none. As an orphan and a foreigner, she lived in disguise, concealing her Jewish identity under Mordecai's instruction.

Each day carried the risk of exposure, rejection, or punishment. Yet she learned to navigate that risk with poise.

By the time she entered the palace, fear had become familiar. What terrified others had become her normal. She lived daily under the tension of secrecy, knowing that one wrong word or gesture could reveal her lineage. Her courage was quiet but consistent. Every day she practiced restraint, self-control, and wisdom.

Her environment demanded maturity long before her age could supply it. No mother to confide in, no father to cry to, and no heritage to publicly claim. She had to depend on intuition and discernment—skills sharpened by survival. Every experience that should have broken her instead built her.

Esther teaches us that courage is often born from loss. When life strips away external security, what remains is inner strength. She became brave not because fear vanished but because she refused to let fear define her. She lived with awareness that fear is a constant reality at every realm of existence, but not everyone becomes a subject of it.

Esther was subjected to fear, yet she never became its subject.

The Mask of Identity

Living in Disguise

Fear thrives in disguise. It hides not only in the shadows of danger but also behind the masks we wear to belong, to succeed, or to survive. For Esther, her disguise was both divine strategy and emotional burden. At Mordecai's instruction, she concealed her Jewish heritage while living within the Persian royal system, carrying the identity of a displaced orphan among the daughters of the land.

Her path to the palace was not a fairy tale. It was a journey through uncertainty, risk, and restrained obedience. When the king's decree went out to gather young women from every province, Esther's inclusion was not a promotion but a conscription. She was taken, not invited.

Brought into a foreign system that prized appearance above authenticity, she learned quickly that favor could be both fragile and fatal.

Under Hegai, the custodian of women, she spent a full year in preparation—six months with oil of myrrh and six with perfumes and cosmetics. Each day was carefully scripted, every movement observed. This was no season of luxury; it was psychological pressure wrapped in fragrance and gold.

Esther had to master composure in an environment where one wrong word, one misplaced expression, or one moment of defiance could cost her everything.

Her concealment was both wisdom and weight. Hiding her heritage meant living in constant awareness that one slip of speech or gesture could expose her. The risk was not only political but existential. To be discovered as Jewish in that environment was to face exclusion, humiliation, or even death.

The crown she eventually wore was not just an emblem of favor; it was a reminder of fragility.

The daily reality of living hidden was exhausting. Fear of exposure breeds restlessness. Esther's silence, though strategic, carried emotional consequences. She lived with the anxiety of double consciousness—always watching, always filtering, always anticipating what could go wrong.

Sleep could not quiet such vigilance. Joy could not fully bloom where self-protection was constant.

This kind of fear is not unique to ancient palaces. Many live the same quiet tension today:

- the professional who conceals faith to keep opportunity
- the woman who masks confidence to appear humble
- the believer who edits convictions to avoid criticism
- the leader who hides vulnerability behind flawless performance

These daily compromises erode peace, replacing authenticity with anxiety. Fear convinces the heart that safety lies in silence.

Esther's life behind the veil of identity was a study in balance. Her survival demanded intelligence, observation, and emotional control. Yet her silence, necessary as it was, also created inner fragmentation.

To live divided between who you are and what you must appear to be is to live in quiet torment.

Every day that Esther woke up in the palace, she faced the unspoken question: *What happens if they know?*

Still, God's hand was working behind her restraint. What felt like a season of concealment was divine preparation. Her silence preserved her until the appointed time.

But there is always a turning point when the cost of hiding outweighs the risk of truth.

The Confrontation

When Silence Becomes Dangerous

But Mordecai was not a gentle mentor. He loved her, but his love carried pressure. When the crisis arose, he appealed not to compassion but to guilt. He said:

"If you remain silent at this time, deliverance will arise from another place… but you and your father's house will perish."

His words were both prophetic and manipulative. He invoked fear of failure to provoke action.

Many live under such relational pressures today. They serve under leaders, parents, supervisors, or mentors who use guilt to motivate obedience. The words may carry truth, but the delivery can feel heavy, coercive, or emotionally unsafe.

Mordecai's urgency was rooted in righteousness, but his method was emotionally forceful.

Esther's response required discernment, not rebellion. She had to obey the divine call without being crushed by human manipulation.

This moment reveals a deeper dimension of courage. Esther was not only confronting national genocide; she was navigating emotional pressure from the only family she had left.

Purpose does not silence fear; it simply gives you something greater to obey.

There are seasons when silence ceases to be wisdom and becomes compromise. Esther realized that to remain quiet was to cooperate with the very system that threatened her people.

Fear tempts us to preserve what purpose calls us to risk.

Her transformation was not emotional—it was spiritual and strategic.

Fasting Before the Throne

Courage Shaped in the Secret Place

The first thing Esther did after accepting her purpose was to call for a fast:

"Go, gather all the Jews in Shushan, and fast for me… And so I will go to the king, which is against the law; and if I perish, I perish."

This was not desperation but preparation.

She understood a timeless principle: **divine outcomes require divine alignment**.

Before confronting the throne of Persia, she approached the throne of grace.

Her fasting was not abstinence—it was alignment.

Courage without communion is noise, but courage shaped by prayer becomes authority.

The Reward of Courage

When Purpose Redefines Power

Every act of obedience carries unseen impact. When Esther stepped out in faith, she not only defied fear; she redefined power.

The king's extended scepter was not mere favor—it was divine validation.

Her courage saved a nation.

But her greatest reward was internal. Fear lost its home in her heart. She no longer performed for acceptance; she lived from divine approval.

Courage, when anchored in purpose, does not just change situations—it changes generations.

Chapter 7 Reflection

---

*"Yet who knows whether you have come to the kingdom for
such a time as this?"*
— *Esther 4:14 (NKJV)*

Awareness

Where have you remained silent, hidden, or hesitant because of
fear—fear of exposure, loss, rejection, or consequence? In what
situations have you chosen safety over obedience, comfort over calling,
or invisibility over influence?

Insight

What did this chapter reveal about how fear can suppress identity
and delay purpose—especially when position is present but courage is
absent? How has fear disguised itself as wisdom, patience, or restraint
while quietly resisting responsibility?

Alignment

Which truth from Esther's moment of decision corrects your
perspective—especially the truth that access without obedience is not
protection, and position without purpose is incomplete?

Action

What specific step of courage will you take this week to stand,
speak, or act—knowing that silence may preserve comfort but
obedience preserves destiny?

Declaration

"I will not allow fear to silence my purpose.

I embrace responsibility with courage and clarity.

I rise to my assignment, positioned by God,

and I respond with obedience for such a time as this."

CHAPTER 8

When Strength Trembles

Paul's Journey with Fear

The Paradox of Fear and Strength

The person of focus in this chapter helps validate one of the most humbling truths about fear: it can attack anyone. Until I began researching for Rx for Fear, my perception of him was that of a fearless, audacious, mountain-moving, territory-shaking man. He was one of my greatest mentors, though I never met him in person. His life impacted me so deeply that I once retraced his footsteps across the places he walked on earth.

Despite years of study and reflection, I had never thought of him as someone who battled fear. My understanding of him was accurate, but through the Rx for Fear lens, I began to see differently. Beneath the strong, intelligent, and strategic leader who outperformed others in his time, at least by his writings, was a man of like passions who faced his own share of fear and panic.

Fear, as I mentioned at the beginning of this book, is an equal opportunity afflicter. Yet what makes this man remarkable is that he acknowledged his fear without shame, without self-condemnation, and without the false humility that often masks insecurity. He wrote with striking honesty, "I was with you in weakness, in fear, and in much trembling" (1 Corinthians 2:3).

Paul—the brilliant theologian, the tireless church planter, the apostle to the Gentiles—confessed that fear was part of his experience, even in ministry. His admission reveals a profound truth: spiritual maturity does not eliminate fear; it reframes it.

Paul understood that human vulnerability was not a disqualification but an invitation to experience grace. His life proves that divine strength often emerges from the soil of human frailty. He shows us that the measure of courage is not in how loudly we speak, but in how honestly we admit our dependence.

Paul's journey introduces us to a different kind of courage—the courage to be honest, the courage to depend, and the courage to surrender. He discovered what many never do: fear is disarmed when weakness meets grace.

The Weight of Paul's World

My understanding of Paul's courage became even clearer when I visited Korinthos. Walking through the archaeological remnants of that ancient city was both enlightening and unsettling. The preserved artifacts from the shrine of Aphrodite revealed a culture steeped in immorality at a level that is difficult to process. I learned how temple slaves were shaven and offered for intimate acts as part of legalized worship. The atmosphere carried the residue of a society where brokenness had been normalized and indulgence was celebrated as spirituality.

Standing there, looking at what remained of the very practices Paul confronted, suddenly his letters took on a new weight. His warnings about the body as the temple of God, his correction of the man who married his father's wife, his passionate plea for purity and holiness—these were not theoretical teachings. They were written into the heart of a culture drowning in darkness.

It was in this environment that Paul admitted, "I was with you in weakness, in fear, and in much trembling." This was not the fear of a timid man. It was the trembling awareness of a messenger carrying holy fire into a city built on sensual worship. It made sense to me in ways I had never considered before. Paul's boldness was shaped in a place where spiritual resistance was palpable. What I saw with my own eyes helped me understand why fear pressed him there, and why grace sustained him.

This experience allows us to connect Paul's world to ours. It validates, with even greater clarity, that fear does not diminish the authenticity of calling. It exposes the depth of the human environment he confronted and gives new meaning to his courage. Paul shows us that even the strongest among us can feel fear, yet still advance with conviction. His life teaches that courage is not the absence of trembling but the decision to move forward under the influence of grace.

A Bridge Between Two Warriors

Standing in Korinthos helped me see Paul in a new light. His fear was not a contradiction to his assignment but a companion that revealed the weight of his environment. And as I reflected on Paul's trembling in Corinth, my heart was drawn back to another man who walked a very different terrain, yet felt fear just as deeply. David and Paul lived centuries apart, served under different covenants, carried different mantles, and faced different enemies. Yet both reveal the same truth.

Fear visits even the chosen, the anointed, the called, and the celebrated.

Paul trembled in a city intoxicated with immorality. David trembled in caves echoing with danger. One faced fear while preaching to a corrupt culture. The other faced fear while running from a murderous king. Their environments were different, but their humanity was the same.

Paul teaches us that fear can accompany purpose. David teaches us that fear can accompany destiny.

Both men reveal that fear does not invalidate the call. It simply exposes our need for the One who sends us. What Paul endured in Corinth sheds light on what David endured in Engedi. Both were navigating psychological, spiritual, and emotional terrains that tested their faith.

This connection prepares us for the journey into David's world, where fear took on multiple forms. By the time we reach Engedi, we discover that fear is not a sign of weakness but a signal that the soul is navigating holy ground.

Just as Paul cried from the tension of ministry, David cried from the edges of survival. And in both cries, we find the same prescription. Trust. Alignment. Grace. Dependence.

Their paths converge in one truth. Fear loses its authority when it meets God.

The Psychology of Fear in Paul

Paul's admission of fear is not the confession of a weak man. It is the confession of a self-aware man. To understand the depth of his trembling in Corinth, we must explore the psychological terrain of his life. Paul did not live in emotional neutrality. He lived in constant tension. His calling exposed him to relentless pressure. His mission placed him in environments that tested his physical endurance, emotional capacity, and spiritual resilience.

Every major psychological factor that activates fear in humans was present in Paul's life. His transparency shows us that fear is not always the result of a lack of faith. Sometimes it is the body's natural response to consistent hardship, threat, trauma, and unpredictability.

1. Paul Experienced Chronic Trauma

Paul lived under the weight of repeated traumatic events. He was beaten, stoned, imprisoned, mobbed, shipwrecked, hunted, and publicly humiliated. The body remembers trauma. Repeated exposure to danger conditions the nervous system to anticipate threat even after the danger has passed. His trembling at Corinth did not mean he lacked faith. It simply meant he had a human nervous system responding to the extreme environments he had survived.

When a person endures prolonged stress, psychological fear becomes intertwined with physical memory. This explains why Paul openly wrote, we were burdened beyond measure, above strength. Trauma magnifies fear by imprinting the body with constant reminders of danger.

2. Paul Lived With Psychological Strain

Paul's assignment demanded constant movement. He was responsible for birthing, nurturing, correcting, and protecting churches across regions that were hostile to the gospel. This level of responsibility creates an invisible strain on the mind. Continual leadership burden can deplete emotional reserves. When he arrived in Corinth, Paul was already carrying the accumulated weight of previous battles.

Corinth was not an easy place. Its spiritual climate alone was enough to overwhelm the mind. When Paul wrote that he was with them in fear and trembling, he was acknowledging the mental fatigue that comes from long-term pressure. Even the strongest minds weaken under sustained load.

3. Paul Faced Social Isolation

True apostleship was lonely work. Paul was often misunderstood, rejected by his own people, resisted by the people he came to help, and abandoned by those he trusted. Social isolation is one of the most powerful triggers of fear. Humans are wired for support. When support is inconsistent, fear grows.

Paul frequently mentioned his need for comfort, companionship, and encouragement. His letters reveal the emotional balancing act of a man who carried the weight of nations on shoulders that often felt alone.

4. Paul Felt the Emotional Burden of Rejection

Rejection is one of the deepest psychological wounds, and Paul experienced it on nearly every missionary journey. The same people he poured himself into were often the ones who questioned his motives, challenged his authority, or misinterpreted his intentions. Rejection attacks identity at its core. Psychological rejection activates the same pain pathways in the brain as physical injury.

Paul's courage should not be measured by how loudly he spoke but by how deeply he felt and still chose to continue.

5. Paul Navigated Continual Uncertainty

One of the most difficult forms of fear is the fear of the unknown. Unpredictability exhausts the mind. Paul never knew what awaited him in the next city. He wrote that he faced danger in rivers, danger among false brethren, danger from citizens, danger from Gentiles. Living in perpetual uncertainty heightens anxiety and magnifies the body's fear response.

Paul lived at the mercy of unpredictable circumstances. The unpredictability alone was enough to activate the amygdala and trigger trembling.

6. Paul Was Not Emotionally Numb

Many assume Paul was emotionally detached because of his intelligence and spiritual stature. The truth is the opposite. Paul was deeply emotional. He felt deeply, loved deeply, and carried others deeply. Emotional sensitivity is a gift, but it also increases vulnerability to fear. He wrote of his internal fears, his burdens for the churches, his sleepless nights, and his tears.

Emotionally sensitive people often experience fear more intensely because they absorb the energy and weight of their environment. Paul was not numb. He was aware. Awareness can feel like weakness, but in Paul's life, it became the doorway to grace.

7. Paul Carried a High Level of Self-Imposed Pressure

Paul's calling was massive. He knew the weight of what he carried. People with high calling often experience the fear of falling short. Paul bore the responsibility of stewarding revelation, planting churches, defending doctrine, and mentoring leaders. The fear of failing God is one of the most psychologically intense fears a believer can carry.

His trembling was not fear of people. It was the shaking of a man who knew the magnitude of what God had entrusted to him. Paul's experience teaches us something essential. Fear is not always evidence of spiritual weakness. Sometimes it is the normal psychological response of a human carrying an extraordinary assignment. His fear did not diminish his calling. It humanized it. And it reveals that God does not require emotional invincibility. He requires surrender.

The Theology of Weakness: My Grace Is Sufficient for You

To understand how Paul processed fear, we must examine the theology that shaped his thinking. Paul did not fight fear through positive thinking or self-elevation. His strength did not come from emotional denial or mental toughness. Paul's stability was anchored in revelation. It was his understanding of weakness that gave him the capacity to function with boldness in environments filled with fear.

God gave Paul a theological foundation that became his psychological anchor.

Paul wrote, "My grace is sufficient for you, for My strength is made perfect in weakness." 2 Corinthians 12:9

This was not encouragement. It was instruction. It was not comfort. It was curriculum. God was teaching Paul a spiritual law. Weakness is not a liability in the kingdom. Weakness is the platform upon which divine strength operates.

1. Weakness Creates Space for Grace

Paul learned that the moments he felt least capable were the very moments when grace was most available. Fear thrives where self-reliance is dominant. Grace flows where self-reliance is surrendered. Paul discovered that emotional trembling was not an indicator that God had left him. It was the signal that grace was about to work.

When fear destabilizes human ability, grace steps into the vacuum.

2. Weakness Exposes Hidden Reliance on Self

One of the deepest forms of fear is the fear of not being enough. Paul had every natural reason to rely on himself. His intellect was unmatched. His training was elite. His revelation was extraordinary. His leadership was exceptional. Yet God allowed him to face situations where all these strengths were insufficient. His trembling in Corinth was not proof of spiritual failure. It was God's way of detoxing him from subtle pride.

Weakness purifies motives. Weakness exposes where trust truly lies.

3. Weakness Forces a Change in Strategy

Fear can cause people to withdraw or resist. Paul responded differently. He allowed weakness to redirect him toward God. Instead of fighting to appear strong, Paul leaned into the vulnerability. He changed his strategy. He stopped depending on eloquence, charisma, and personality, and chose instead to depend on the power of God.

He wrote to the Corinthians that his preaching was not with persuasive words of human wisdom but in demonstration of the Spirit and power. Weakness made him shift from human effort to divine manifestation.

4. Weakness Becomes a Tool for Humility and Balance

Paul was entrusted with revelations that no man had carried before him. High revelation requires deep humility. God allowed weakness to remain as a balancing tool. It kept Paul grounded. It kept him compassionate. It kept him relatable. Weakness gave him the ability to feel what others felt and to minister from a place of connection rather than superiority.

Weakness made Paul wise. Weakness made Paul balanced.

5. Weakness Makes Grace Visible

Grace is invisible until weakness creates an opportunity for it to be seen. Paul's fear, trembling, and emotional transparency allowed the power of God to be displayed through him. His vulnerability made his ministry accessible. People did not follow Paul because he was invincible. They followed him because he was surrendered.

Weakness is the magnifying glass through which the strength of God becomes visible.

6. Weakness Transforms Fear Into Spiritual Authority

Paul learned that fear loses its power in the presence of revelation. The moment he understood that God specializes in making strength out of weakness, his trembling no longer threatened him. He stopped fighting fear and started reframing it. His authority came not from being fearless but from being aligned with grace.

When weakness becomes understood, fear becomes disarmed.

7. Weakness Teaches Trust at the Deepest Level

The theology of weakness is essentially a theology of trust. Paul learned that trust is not the absence of fear. Trust is the decision to keep moving when fear is present. Trust is the choice to lean into God when the body wants to retreat. Trust is the posture that turns weakness into worship.

Paul stopped asking for the removal of weakness. He started embracing it as the place where grace works best. Weakness is not a problem God wants to eliminate. It is the place where He wants to manifest His strength.

Grace is not a theological concept. It is God's active response to human limitation.

Paul's Prescriptions for Conquering Fear

Paul did not overcome fear by accident. He overcame it through practice. His life reveals a pattern of spiritual habits, mental disciplines, and emotional strategies that formed a complete prescription for fear. These prescriptions were not theoretical. They were survival strategies. They were the tools that allowed him to stand in hostile cities, endure physical attacks, face emotional betrayal, and continue ministering with unwavering conviction.

Paul did not remove fear. He regulated it. He redirected it. He reframed it. He overcame fear by developing rhythms that kept his spirit aligned, his mind renewed, and his emotions stable.

1. The Prescription of Prayer

Paul prayed constantly. Prayer was not an event for him. It was a lifestyle. It was the spiritual oxygen that kept his inner world steady. Prayer did not always remove the danger around him, but it removed the panic within him. Prayer anchored his mind and aligned his heart.

He wrote that he prayed without ceasing. He prayed in prisons. He prayed in storms. He prayed in weakness. Prayer was the space where his trembling met divine comfort.

Prayer was his emotional stabilizer.

2. The Prescription of Perspective Renewal

Paul's greatest battles were not external. They were internal. He fought fear by renewing his perspective. He practiced the discipline of reframing. When life pressed him, he shifted his interpretation. He reframed prison as purpose. He reframed weakness as strength. He reframed hardship as preparation. He reframed suffering as spiritual gain.

He wrote that the light afflictions of the present time are working for us a far more exceeding weight of glory. That is reframing. That is spiritual cognitive renewal.

Perspective determines response. When Paul changed the meaning of his trials, the fear attached to them lost force.

3. The Prescription of Worship

Worship was Paul's therapy. In the prison at Philippi, he sang until the atmosphere changed. Worship resets the nervous system. Worship interrupts negative emotional cycles. Worship shifts the mind from fear to focus.

Worship is not music. It is surrender. Paul used worship to regulate fear and restore the awareness of God's presence. Worship turns fear into reverence.

Worship was his spiritual regulation tool.

4. The Prescription of Honest Expression

Paul never suppressed his emotions. He expressed them. He acknowledged them. He named them. Emotional honesty is one of the greatest tools for conquering fear. What is acknowledged can be healed. What is hidden becomes toxic.

Paul wrote of sorrow, despair, weakness, tears, and trembling. Emotional transparency prevented emotional overload. Fear grows in silence. Paul confronted it with expression.

Honest language created inner clarity.

5. The Prescription of Community and Support

Although Paul carried a heavy assignment, he understood the value of support. He surrounded himself with companions who strengthened him emotionally and spiritually. Luke, Timothy, Barnabas, Silas, Titus, and others were not simply coworkers. They were emotional anchors.

Fear intensifies in isolation. Community reduces its power. Paul sought comfort from friends and expressed gratitude for their presence. Partnership was part of his healing.

Support gave him psychological stability.

6. The Prescription of Mental Focus

Paul practiced disciplined thinking. He refused to allow fear to dominate his imagination. He trained his mind toward purity, truth, hope, and virtue. He instructed believers to think on things that are noble, just, pure, and praiseworthy. This instruction was born from his own practice.

Mental focus is a weapon. A wandering mind is fertile ground for fear. Paul guarded his thoughts with intentionality.

His focus redirected emotional energy.

7. The Prescription of Identity Consciousness

Perhaps Paul's strongest weapon against fear was identity. Paul never forgot who he was in Christ. He consistently reaffirmed his identity in every letter. Chosen. Called. Appointed. Sealed. Strengthened. Delivered. Redeemed.

Identity is the anchor of emotional resilience. When fear attacks identity, courage collapses. Paul reinforced his identity through confession, remembrance, and revelation.

Identity consciousness made him immovable.

8. The Prescription of Dependence on the Spirit

Paul depended on the Spirit for strength, clarity, courage, and comfort. Human strength cannot confront spiritual fear. Only spiritual empowerment can. He wrote that the Spirit helps our weaknesses. He taught that those who walk in the Spirit overcome the limits of the flesh.

Fear loses its voice where the Spirit becomes the source of confidence.

Dependence transformed his trembling into tenacity.

Paul overcame fear through spiritual rhythm, mental focus, emotional honesty, and continuous surrender. His prescriptions are not formulas but patterns. They teach us that fear can be managed, restrained, redirected, and defeated through consistent alignment with God.

Fear cannot dominate where prayer is constant. Fear cannot cripple where identity is secure. Fear cannot destroy where grace is active. Fear cannot remain where the Spirit is present.

Paul did not survive ministry because he was fearless. He survived because he was disciplined.

Paul's Darkest Days: When Life Itself Felt Too Heavy

There is a moment in Paul's writings that exposes the deepest layer of fear. It is the kind of fear that pushes a person beyond trembling and into the realm of emotional collapse. It is the fear that sits in the human spirit when life feels unbearable. Paul did not hide this moment. He recorded it so that generations would know that even the strongest saints can be pressed beyond their limits.

He wrote these words with startling honesty.

"We were burdened beyond measure, above strength, so that we despaired even of life itself." 2 Corinthians 1:8

This was not the language of a tired preacher. It was the confession of a man drowning under pressure. The word despaired reveals the emotional depth of his suffering. In the original language it means to be utterly without a solution, unable to see a way forward, trapped between responsibility and reality.

Paul reached a moment where the emotional and spiritual toll of his assignment exceeded the capacity of his humanity.

1. The Breaking Point of a Chosen Vessel

Paul was not a fragile man. He endured more suffering than many will face in ten lifetimes. Yet even he reached a breaking point. This moment reveals that the presence of fear and despair does not indicate absence of faith. It reveals the limits of the human frame.

His despair was not rebellion. It was exhaustion. It was the moment where internal stress collided with external pressure and produced emotional collapse.

Paul was honest about it. That honesty becomes a revelation. It is possible to be chosen and still be overwhelmed. It is possible to be anointed and still be afraid. It is possible to be called and still feel like quitting. Paul suffered these emotions so that we would know that being overwhelmed does not disqualify a believer. It makes us human.

2. The Pain Behind the Ministry

Paul's dark moment did not come from laziness or neglect. It came from overextension, persecution, emotional fatigue, physical danger, relational tension, and spiritual warfare. Ministry at this level took a toll on his body, mind, and emotions.

Repeated beatings, stonings, imprisonments, sleepless nights, hunger, betrayal, false accusations, shipwrecks, and constant travel created emotional depletion. Trauma accumulates. Stress accumulates. Fear accumulates. The body can only absorb so much before the soul begins to tremble.

Paul was not weak. He was overloaded.

3. The Fear of Unknown Outcomes

In this season Paul could not predict the future. Every city carried danger. Every journey carried risk. Every decision carried weight. He lived with the continual uncertainty of what would come next. Unpredictability is one of the strongest psychological triggers of fear.

Fear thrives where outcomes are unclear. Paul experienced the internal panic that rises when the human mind cannot find safety or certainty.

He was a brilliant man, yet intelligence was not enough to silence fear. He was a spiritual giant, yet anointing did not remove the pressure. He was a leader, yet responsibility intensified his emotional burden.

4. The Crisis of Internal Pressure

Paul wrote that he was burdened beyond strength. This phrase reveals the internal collapse of a man who had reached emotional capacity. There are seasons when internal pressure becomes more dangerous than external attack. Internal pressure drains motivation. It drains hope. It drains perspective.

Fear becomes heavier when the body is tired, the emotions are stretched, and the mind is overwhelmed. Paul's confession shows that even the strongest are vulnerable to internal collapse.

5. The Despair That Brings Transformation

Paul's despair was not wasted. It became the doorway to a revelation of trust. In the next verse he wrote that this despair happened so that he would not trust in himself but in God who raises the dead. Despair stripped him of self-reliance. Fear exposed the limits of the flesh. Weakness revealed the need for deeper dependence.

Paul learned that when life feels too heavy, God becomes the strength that carries it.

His darkest moment became the framework for one of the strongest revelations of his ministry. It produced a theology of trust that changed how he taught, how he led, and how he endured.

6. The Courage to Continue After Collapse

The miracle in Paul's story is not simply that he survived. The miracle is that he continued. Many people never recover after emotional collapse. Many lose their drive, their creativity, their courage, and their desire to try again. Paul rose from despair with a deeper understanding of grace.

He realized that emotional collapse is not final. It is the invitation to rebuild with God's strength. He continued his journey with the knowledge that he was not carrying the weight of his calling alone.

The same man who once despaired of life later wrote that he could do all things through Christ who strengthened him.

Paul teaches us that despair is not always failure. Sometimes it is the breaking point that births a new dimension of trust. It is the moment where human strength ends and divine strength begins. Fear loses its ability to dominate when we understand that even in emotional collapse, grace is still active.

Fear may overwhelm, but it cannot overthrow the believer who learns to trust God in weakness.

Chapter 8 Reflection

"And I was with you in weakness, in fear, and in much trembling."
— *1 Corinthians 2:3 (NKJV)*

Awareness

Where do you currently feel weak, overwhelmed, or emotionally stretched beyond your capacity? In what environments or responsibilities do you experience pressure similar to what Paul faced in Corinth—moments that provoke anxiety, trembling, or inner instability?

Where have prolonged stress, leadership weight, or constant responsibility quietly eroded your emotional strength? Do you acknowledge these moments honestly, or do you hide fear behind performance, productivity, or spiritual language?

Insight

What did this chapter reveal about the nature of fear when it intersects with calling and responsibility? How does Paul's transparency challenge the belief that fear disqualifies strength or spiritual authority?

In what ways has fear in your life been fueled by exhaustion, emotional strain, internal pressure, or unrealistic expectations rather than lack of faith? How has fear spoken lies about your capacity, your assignment, or your identity?

Alignment

Which truth from Paul's experience corrects how you interpret fear—especially the truth that fear acknowledged is not weakness, and vulnerability surrendered becomes a doorway for grace?

How does the reality that God's power is revealed through dependence—not self-reliance—reframe how you view your current season?

Action

What intentional step will you take this week to respond to fear with grace rather than resistance? This may include rest, prayer, perspective renewal, honest conversation, community support, worship, or releasing unrealistic expectations.

What practical rhythm can you establish to ensure strength flows from alignment rather than striving?

Declaration

"I acknowledge my humanity without shame. I refuse to interpret fear as failure or weakness. God has given me power, love, and a sound mind. I receive grace for every trembling moment. I am strengthened from within. My mind is steady, my heart is aligned, and my spirit is anchored in truth. Where fear once ruled, peace now reigns."

CHAPTER 9

Storm-Induced Fear

The Disciples in the Boat

Fear has many expressions, but few are as sudden or as destabilizing as the fear that erupts in crisis. It is the fear that strikes without warning, invading familiar spaces and turning routine moments into scenes of panic. This is the kind of fear that exposes what we truly trust and what we merely assume we believe.

The storm on the Sea of Galilee is one of the clearest biblical portraits of fear under pressure. These were not inexperienced men. The disciples were professional fishermen who understood the rhythms, moods, and dangers of that sea. Yet the storm they faced that night was unlike anything they were prepared for. What they expected to control suddenly controlled them. What they believed was predictable became violently unpredictable. The familiar became frightening.

Crisis does that. It interrupts life without notice, strips away the illusion of mastery, and confronts us with the truth that fear does not always arise from the unknown. Sometimes it is the familiar that turns against us.

Mark's account reveals not only the force of the storm but also the internal storm inside the disciples. Their panic distorted perception. Their minds shifted into survival mode. Their fear magnified danger and minimized divine presence. Their words reflected a mind overwhelmed by anxiety: "Teacher, do You not care that we are perishing?" Panic convinced them that Jesus' silence meant abandonment.

Yet what looked like danger was actually a classroom. Jesus used the storm not to destroy them but to train them. He allowed the crisis to reveal the hidden state of their faith, their dependence, their emotional limits, and their instinctive reactions under pressure. The storm was not only a physical event; it was a diagnostic tool.

Fear in crisis exposes where faith resides. It uncovers the tension between what we confess and what we believe. It reveals whether peace is anchored in circumstances or in the presence of Christ.

Psychologically, the disciples' reaction mirrors the human fight or flight response. In moments of threat, the brain floods the body with adrenaline and cortisol, narrowing focus to danger and shutting down logical reasoning. Anxiety distorts perception. Panic silences memory. Fear convinces the heart that survival is more important than truth.

But Jesus slept through what terrified them. His posture was not indifference but instruction. He demonstrated what emotional regulation looks like when anchored in divine assurance. He invited them into a new way of seeing, thinking, and responding.

This chapter explores the anatomy of storm induced fear and how Jesus used crisis to cultivate resilience. The storm was not a punishment but a pathway to revelation. The fear it triggered became the doorway to deeper trust.

What shook them was the very place Christ intended to strengthen them.

Fear in the Familiar – Storms That Catch Us Off Guard

Fear becomes most unsettling when it rises in places we trust. The disciples did not encounter this storm in unfamiliar territory. Although they were not all fishermen, the most prominent and experienced among them were. Peter, Andrew, James, and John had spent much of their lives on the Sea of Galilee. They understood its rhythms, its winds, and its unpredictable moods. For them, this sea was not simply water; it was a workplace, a comfort zone, and an environment where their skills gave them confidence. Yet the storm they faced that night defied every ability they possessed.

This is what makes storm induced fear so destabilizing. It strikes where confidence is supposed to reside. It challenges our assumptions about what we believe we have mastered. It disrupts areas of competence and exposes vulnerabilities we did not know we carried. Nothing shakes us like crisis in the familiar.

Many people can manage adversity in places where they expect it. Challenges from enemies can be anticipated. Difficulties in new assignments can be prepared for. But when trouble rises in the ordinary spaces of life, the shock is deeper. When a marriage that felt stable suddenly enters turbulence, the heart panics. When a child who has never given cause for concern begins to struggle, fear multiplies. When a steady job dissolves without warning, the ground beneath feels unsafe. When health issues arise from nowhere, even the strongest lose balance.

These are storms that catch us off guard. They do not ask for permission. They do not respect preparation. They reveal that predictability is not the same as security.

The disciples began that evening with confidence. Jesus had said, "Let us cross over to the other side." These words should have anchored their faith, yet the storm erased their memory of His instruction. Crisis can silence the very promises meant to sustain us. Storms have the ability to override what we know and activate fear we did not realize was dormant.

In familiar places, fear feels more personal. It is not just the wind and waves that intimidate; it is the sense of betrayal by the environment we trusted. The disciples had likely crossed this lake countless times.

Their experience gave them a sense of control. Crisis shattered that expectation.

There is also a hidden psychological dimension. Fear in the familiar triggers a deeper sense of violation. It creates cognitive dissonance. The mind fights to reconcile what it knows with what it sees, and when it cannot, panic takes over. Familiarity ceases to comfort and becomes a reminder of lost control.

God allows storms in familiar places for a reason. They expose our dependence on routine rather than relationship. They show us how often we trust predictability instead of divine presence. They reveal whether our confidence is built on skill or instruction, on environment or on Christ.

The disciples were not wrong for being afraid, but they were unprepared for what God intended to teach them. The storm was not designed to drown them but to develop them. It was meant to shift their confidence from what they knew to whom they followed. The familiar had to be shaken so that their faith could be strengthened.

Storms in familiar places remind us that security is not found in experience but in Jesus. He is the anchor that holds when everything we know feels unstable.

The Physiology of Panic

Panic is not just emotional; it is physiological. It is the body's immediate response to perceived danger. The disciples' reaction in the storm mirrors this biological process with startling accuracy. One moment they were rowing with confidence, and the next they were fighting for survival. Their breathing quickened, their voices rose, and their judgment collapsed under the weight of urgency. Panic took over before faith could speak.

When the brain senses threat, the amygdala sends an alarm throughout the nervous system. Adrenaline floods the bloodstream.

The heart races. Breathing becomes shallow and rapid. Muscles tighten. Vision narrows. The body prepares for fight or flight long before the mind has time to reason. This is why panic often feels uncontrollable. It is the body reacting faster than the brain can interpret.

In that moment on the sea, the disciples were not thinking clearly. Their words revealed it: "Teacher, do You not care that we are perishing?" Panic convinced them that God's presence in the boat was irrelevant. It distorted their perception, magnifying danger and minimizing divine proximity. The storm outside triggered a storm inside, and their physiology drowned out their theology.

This is the nature of panic. It makes the heart forget what the mind once knew. It silences memory. It clouds judgment. It rewrites reality. Under panic, even truth feels distant. The disciples had seen Jesus heal the sick, raise the dead, cast out demons, and speak with authority. Yet the shock of the storm activated a fear that overpowered their memory of His power.

Modern psychology describes this as cognitive distortion. In a heightened state, the mind interprets danger in extremes. Thoughts become inflated. Risks appear larger than they are. Worst case scenarios take center stage. This is why the disciples did not simply say, "This storm is dangerous." They said, "We are perishing." Panic bypassed possibility and moved straight to catastrophe.

Panic also triggers emotional reasoning. Feelings become facts. The disciples felt abandoned; therefore they concluded that Jesus did not care. This happens to many today. Panic makes the silence of God feel like neglect. It turns delays into denials and stillness into indifference. Yet in reality, God was not absent. He was resting. His rest was a revelation, not a rejection.

There is also a spiritual layer. Panic invites doubt to sit where faith once ruled. It creates space for fear to interpret circumstances through a lens of defeat. The disciples were in the presence of Peace Himself, yet panic made them believe they were alone. Fear always fights to separate perception from truth.

The storm revealed something deeper than the disciples' fear of drowning. It exposed their lack of emotional regulation. They knew how to handle water as fishermen, but they did not yet know how to handle fear as followers. Their hearts had not been trained to stay steady under pressure. Their bodies responded faster than their beliefs. Their physiology drowned their faith.

Jesus understood this. Before He addressed their theology, He confronted their fear. Before He corrected their lack of faith, He calmed their nervous system by calming the sea. He spoke peace to the environment so they could regain clarity within themselves.

This is a profound revelation. The God who created our emotions also understands the biology behind them. His commands, His presence, and His peace address both the spiritual and the physical. He does not shame us for panic; He meets us in it.

Panic may be a natural human response, but it is not meant to govern the believer. Jesus allows storms not to activate fear but to reveal where fear resides and where faith must grow.

The Master in the Midst of Chaos

One of the greatest revelations in this story is not the severity of the storm but the posture of Jesus during the storm. While the disciples were fighting for their lives, Jesus was asleep. His tranquility in the midst of chaos was not indifference; it was instruction. His rest revealed the strength of His internal world. What terrified them could not trouble Him.

Jesus was in the same boat, facing the same waves, hearing the same wind, and feeling the same violent rocking of the vessel. Yet His response was completely different. He slept. His rest was not careless; it was confident. It was the assurance that the presence of danger does not determine destiny. His posture declared a truth the disciples had not yet learned. Peace is not the absence of storms but the presence of trust.

To the disciples, His sleep felt like neglect. Crisis often makes us misinterpret divine posture. Silence feels like abandonment. Stillness feels like distance. Rest feels like disinterest. Yet Jesus was teaching them something they could not learn on calm waters. He was showing them the kind of faith that does not panic when conditions shift.

Jesus was not asleep because He lacked awareness. He was asleep because He possessed authority. While the disciples reacted to what they saw, Jesus rested in what He knew. This difference is the foundation of emotional regulation in the believer's life. Fear reacts to circumstances. Faith rests in truth.

There is also a psychological dimension. Christ's posture represented emotional stability. He demonstrated the power of a regulated nervous system. While the disciples' adrenaline surged, His remained calm. His sleep was a picture of what happens when peace governs the internal world. He modeled what it looks like when emotions submit to divine identity rather than external conditions.

The disciples woke Him with desperation, saying, "Teacher, do You not care that we are perishing?" Their cry revealed more than fear; it revealed misunderstanding. They questioned His care because they could not interpret His calm. They assumed that if He cared, He would panic with them. Many believers fall into this same pattern. We measure God's involvement by emotional expression rather than by divine presence.

But Jesus cared enough to rest. His calm was intentional. His posture was prophetic. He was inviting them to rise to the level of His peace. Instead of matching their panic, He demonstrated what authority looks like under pressure. By sleeping, Jesus confronted their belief that safety depends on control. He showed them that safety depends on who is in the boat.

He did not ask them why they did not wake Him sooner. He did not rebuke them for seeking His help. He rebuked the storm, and then He addressed the condition of their hearts. This order matters. Jesus calmed the environment before correcting the internal environment. He restored external peace so they could listen. He addressed fear only after addressing danger.

In crisis, Jesus remains exactly who He has always been: Master, Teacher, and Peace. He is never overwhelmed by what overwhelms us. He sits within the storm with authority that cannot be shaken. His presence is the anchor that holds when everything else begins to sink.

This is the revelation the disciples needed to carry into their future. Ministry would not always happen on calm shores. They would face persecution, imprisonment, opposition, and hardship. Their ability to lead would depend on their ability to rest in the character of Christ. The storm was preparation for future pressure. The boat became their first classroom on emotional resilience.

Jesus taught them that chaos is not a sign of divine absence. It is a stage for divine revelation. Fear may enter the boat, but so does the Master. His presence is the regulator that stabilizes the soul.

Peace, Be Still – The Voice That Regulates Fear

When Jesus finally rose to address the storm, He did not match the disciples' panic. He did not shout over the wind in fear or react to the waves in distress. His authority was calm. His command was simple. He spoke two words that carried the weight of creation: "Peace, be still." What terrified them submitted instantly. The unrest of nature bowed to the rest of its Creator.

Jesus did not speak to the disciples first. He spoke to the storm. He confronted the environment before confronting their emotions. This order is significant. There are moments when the external pressure is so loud that the heart cannot hear instruction. So Jesus quieted the sea to quiet their nervous system. He calmed the world around them so they could receive truth within them.

He addressed the wind and the waves with authority because He understood that fear had been triggered by what they saw. He removed the source of their panic to help them regain clarity. This is a picture of divine compassion. God does not only speak to the heart; He also speaks to the circumstances that overwhelm the heart.

"Peace, be still" is more than a command to nature. It is a command to the soul. It is the voice that regulates fear. The same power that calmed the sea can calm the mind. The same authority that subdued the storm can subdue anxiety. Jesus showed that peace is not something we create. It is something He speaks.

There is also psychological insight in His approach. When panic floods the body, rational thinking becomes inaccessible. The brain shifts into survival mode. The nervous system overrides reasoning. Jesus calmed the external storm to deactivate the disciples' internal alarm system. He reset their physiological response so that faith could breathe again.

Once the sea was still, He turned to them and asked, "Why are you so fearful? How is it that you have no faith?" These questions were not shaming. They were diagnostic. He did not ask, "Why did you wake Me?" or "Why did you disturb My sleep?" He asked, "Why are you afraid?" because He was exposing the deeper issue. Their fear was not caused by the storm. Their fear was caused by their unbelief.

Storms do not create fear. They reveal it. Crisis exposes the fault lines in our faith. It shows where we rely on experience instead of instruction, where we lean on skill instead of Scripture, and where we trust familiarity more than divine presence.

When Jesus said, "Peace, be still," He also taught them something profound. Peace is not a feeling. Peace is a Person. It is the presence of Christ that stabilizes the soul. His voice regulates fear the way a physician regulates heart rhythm. His words align the internal world. His authority resets emotional balance.

This revelation was meant to stay with them. They would face many storms in the future, some physical and many spiritual. Persecution, imprisonment, accusation, and opposition would come. But this moment would remind them that the same voice that calmed the sea could calm their spirits. They would learn to hear "Peace, be still" even when Jesus was not physically in the boat.

For every believer, the same truth applies. Christ still speaks peace into chaos. He still regulates fear by His word. He still calms storms so we can regain clarity. And He still asks the same question: "Why are you afraid?"

Not to condemn us, but to awaken us. Not to shame us, but to strengthen us. Not to expose weakness, but to reveal where trust must grow.

His voice is the difference between drowning in panic and rising in faith.

Faith That Sleeps Through Storms

The greatest miracle in this story is not the calming of the wind or the silencing of the sea. It is the revelation that faith can learn to rest in the middle of a storm. Jesus did not simply stop the chaos. He modeled a completely different response to it. His sleep was the lesson. His rest was the revelation. His posture became the blueprint for a mature believer.

Faith that sleeps through storms is not denial. It is not irresponsibility. It is not avoidance. It is a settled confidence that the presence of Christ is greater than the pressure of crisis. It is the internal assurance that God does not abandon His word just because circumstances become violent. The disciples had His instruction: "Let us cross over to the other side." That word should have governed their emotions. Instead, the storm drowned their memory of His promise.

Faith that sleeps trusts the promise more than the problem.

Jesus wanted to elevate their understanding of faith from reaction to rest. He wanted them to see that authority is not proven in panic. It is demonstrated in peace. He wanted them to know that spiritual maturity is not measured by the absence of storms but by stability within them.

There is also a psychological dimension. Rest is a form of emotional regulation. It signals to the nervous system that there is no threat. When Jesus slept, He was modeling the conditioning of a regulated mind. The disciples' bodies were in chaos because their minds were overwhelmed. Jesus' body rested because His mind was anchored. He was not governed by adrenaline, fear, or urgency. He was governed by identity.

Faith that sleeps becomes possible when the internal world refuses to be defined by the external world. It is the kind of faith that understands that storms may be strong, but the One who speaks to storms is stronger. It is the kind of faith that anchors itself in truth even when sight is disturbed. It is the kind of faith that believes the journey will not end in death because Jesus initiated it.

When the storm ceased and the sea became calm, the disciples were filled with a new kind of fear. Scripture says, "They feared exceedingly and said to one another, 'Who can this be, that even the wind and the sea obey Him?'" Their fear shifted from danger to reverence. It was no longer storm induced fear. It was awe. This shift is significant. Storms that once terrified them now opened their eyes to divine authority.

Fear was not removed. It was redirected.

This is the transformation Jesus desired. He wanted their fear to evolve into worship. He wanted their panic to mature into reverence.

He wanted them to understand that fear of circumstances must bow to fear of the Lord. The storm had to break their confidence in their own ability so they could develop confidence in His identity.

Faith that sleeps through storms becomes possible when we trust who is in the boat more than what is happening around the boat. It grows as we learn to rehearse truth rather than react to turbulence. It strengthens as we learn to interpret circumstances through the lens of divine presence rather than through the lens of fear.

This kind of faith is not born in calm seasons. It is formed in storms. It is shaped when God allows conditions that challenge our assumptions and unsettle our predictability. It is refined when the familiar is shaken and the heart must choose between fear and trust.

The disciples entered the boat as fishermen. They left as students of divine peace.

Storms will come, but the believer who learns to rest in the character of Christ can walk through crisis with calm that confuses the enemy. Faith that sleeps through storms reveals a soul that is anchored not in circumstances but in God.

Chapter 9 Reflection

"But He said to them, 'Why are you fearful, O you of little faith?' Then He arose and rebuked the winds and the sea, and there was a great calm."
— *Matthew 8:26 (NKJV)*

Awareness

Storms do not always arise in unfamiliar territory. Often, they erupt in places we assumed were mastered—areas of routine, experience, or perceived control. The disciples were not novices at sea, yet fear overtook them.

Where in your life has something familiar recently become unstable or unpredictable? Which roles, routines, or identities have you relied on for security rather than God's presence? When pressure intensifies, which emotion surfaces first—panic, anger, withdrawal, or emotional numbness?

Insight

What did this chapter reveal about the nature of panic—especially how fear accelerates faster than reason and distorts perception? How does the disciples' reaction expose the human tendency to interpret God's silence as absence?

In what ways has fear narrowed your vision, causing truth to feel distant and danger to feel absolute? How has emotional intensity overridden spiritual memory in moments of crisis?

"Fear can make truth feel unreal and make danger feel absolute."

Alignment

Which truth from this chapter realigns your understanding— especially the truth that Christ's presence is not invalidated by His silence? How does knowing that Jesus was in the boat, even while asleep, reshape how you interpret your current storm?

What does it mean for your heart to return to rest rather than reaction?

"In returning and rest you shall be saved; In quietness and confidence shall be your strength." — *Isaiah 30:15 (NKJV)*

Action

What intentional step will you take this week to allow Christ to regulate the storm within you? This may include slowing your pace, practicing stillness, regulating your breath, or consciously shifting focus from circumstance to presence.

Practice this moment of recalibration:

- Inhale slowly.
- Invite the Holy Spirit into the area of fear.
- Whisper: *"Jesus, speak peace over me."*

What practical rhythm can you establish to preserve emotional rest when life feels unstable?

Declaration

"I refuse to interpret God's silence as absence.
Christ is in my boat, and I will not be moved.
Peace is my portion because His presence surrounds me.
My faith rests even when waves rise.
The One who commands the winds commands my heart."

"You will keep him in perfect peace,
Whose mind is stayed on You,
Because he trusts in You."
— *Isaiah 26:3 (NKJV)*

CHAPTER 10

Healing Fear in the Body and Mind

Science & Scripture

Fear is not only spiritual. It is also physical, neurological, and deeply embodied. Long before we can name what we feel, the body reacts. The heart races. The chest tightens. The mind spirals. The nervous system braces for impact. Fear does not simply visit the mind; it imprints itself on the body.

Scripture acknowledges this truth in ways that modern science is only beginning to articulate. David wrote, "My heart is severely pained within me" in Psalm 55, a description that mirrors the symptoms of acute anxiety. In Psalm 46, God responds with an invitation that calms the body as much as the soul: "Be still, and know that I am God." Stillness is not passive. It is a spiritual and physiological intervention. It slows the breath, quiets the heart, and restores internal balance.

This chapter explores the intersection of science and Scripture, showing how both work together to heal fear. God designed the human body with systems that respond to threat, and He provided spiritual tools that regulate those systems. Worship calms the nervous system. Music rewires emotional pathways. Journaling releases internal tension. Reflection reorders thought. Prayer shifts focus and restores clarity. These practices are not random. They are therapeutic. They are divine strategies for managing fear.

David, one of the most emotionally expressive figures in Scripture, instinctively used these tools. His psalms were not simply songs. They were therapy sessions. When he played music for Saul, it eased the king's torment and quieted his anxiety. When David poured out his heart in writing, he was practicing what modern psychology calls expressive journaling, a method proven to reduce anxiety and improve emotional resilience. His tears, his worship, his cries, and his reflections were not signs of weakness. They were pathways to healing.

Science now affirms what Scripture revealed centuries ago. The brain renews itself through meditation. The body heals through emotional expression. Music regulates the vagus nerve. Gratitude rewires neural pathways. Stillness reduces cortisol. Prayer lowers stress and enhances mental clarity. What God commanded for spiritual well-being also produces biological well-being.

Healing fear requires harmony between the nervous system and the soul. Fear is felt in the body, processed in the mind, and healed in the spirit. The path to wholeness cannot ignore any of these dimensions. God uses worship to stabilize the emotions, truth to correct distorted thinking, expression to relieve internal pressure, and rest to restore the entire system.

This chapter will help you understand fear not only as a feeling but as a physical experience. It will show you how God integrates science and Scripture to bring comfort, clarity, and calm. It will also reveal that the practices David used for survival are the same practices God invites us to use today for emotional and spiritual restoration.

Healing begins when we stop ignoring what the body is expressing and allow the soul to release what it has been holding.

The Biology of Fear – What Happens Inside the Body

Fear is not only a feeling. It is a full-body experience. Long before the mind understands what is happening, the body reacts. The moment the brain perceives danger, real or imagined, it sends an alarm through the entire nervous system. This is why fear can feel overwhelming even when circumstances do not justify the intensity. The body often remembers what the mind has not yet processed.

At the center of this response is a small almond-shaped structure in the brain called the amygdala. It functions as the security guard of the nervous system. The amygdala scans for threat and reacts instantly. It does not ask for permission. It does not wait for logic. It moves faster than conscious thought. When it senses danger, it activates the fight or flight response.

The heart begins to race. Breathing becomes shallow. Muscles tighten. The stomach churns. The voice trembles. The mind narrows to a single focus: survival. This reaction is automatic. It is God-designed. It protects the body from harm when quick decisions matter. But it also causes distress when fear is rooted in memory, imagination, or emotional pain rather than physical threat.

This is why the body can respond to internal fears as if they were external dangers. Stressful thoughts can cause the same rise in heart rate that physical danger does. Traumatic memories can create the same tension in the muscles as a present threat. Worry can produce the same fatigue as physical exertion. The body does not always distinguish between danger and discomfort.

David described this experience in Psalm 55. He said, "My heart is severely pained within me, and the terrors of death have fallen upon me." His language mirrors what modern psychology now calls panic. His chest tightened. His thoughts raced. His body reacted intensely to emotional danger. Scripture recognizes the biological reality of fear long before science assigned names to it.

Yet the biology is only one side of the experience. The problem is not that the body reacts. The problem is when the body stays in reaction. Prolonged fear keeps the nervous system in a constant state of alert. Cortisol remains elevated. Muscles remain tense. Sleep becomes disrupted. Rest becomes difficult. The body operates as if danger is always near, even when life is calm.

This is where spiritual practices become essential. Stillness slows the breath and signals safety. Worship lowers stress hormones and releases emotional tension. Prayer shifts attention from fear to faith. Meditation on Scripture rewires thought patterns and engages parts of the brain associated with peace. These are not merely devotional activities. They are interventions.

God designed the body to respond to danger, but He also designed the soul to regulate the body. The Spirit calms the mind. The mind calms the body. When the inner world comes into agreement with truth, the nervous system begins to recover.

Understanding the biology of fear does not diminish its spiritual reality. It simply reminds us that fear touches every part of who we are. It explains why the psalmist cried, why his bones felt weak, and why his strength drained under emotional pressure. It also explains why God often begins healing with rest, stillness, and reassurance.

Fear affects the brain, the heart, the breath, the muscles, and the hormones. Healing must therefore address the whole person. The same God who formed the nervous system also formed the pathways of peace. His command, "Be still," is not poetic. It is physiological. It quiets the body so the soul can hear again.

Fear may begin in the body, but it does not have to end there.

The Spirit of Peace and the Mind of Christ

Fear does not only attack the body. It also wages war against the mind. When fear is left unchallenged, it distorts perception, magnifies threat, and weakens decision making. Scripture calls this a troubled mind, a restless mind, or a mind weighed down. Yet God has given every believer access to a different mental atmosphere. Paul called it the mind of Christ.

The mind of Christ is not simply a spiritual concept. It is a state of clarity, order, and peace that regulates thought and anchors emotion.

It is the posture of a heart that trusts God even when circumstances are uncertain. It is the capacity to interpret life through truth rather than through fear. This is why Philippians 4:7 says that the peace of God will guard the heart and mind. Peace is not only comfort. It is protection.

Modern neuroscience explains this process with remarkable detail. When thoughts are anxious, the amygdala becomes overactive. When thoughts are grounded in truth, the prefrontal cortex takes the lead and calms the emotional centers. In other words, what we meditate on shapes our emotional world. What we focus on becomes the atmosphere of our mind.

Scripture confirms this. Romans 12:2 instructs us to be transformed by the renewing of the mind. Renewal is not a single moment. It is a repeated practice of replacing fearful thoughts with divine truth. It is the discipline of aligning mental patterns with God's perspective. Over time, this alignment creates stability. It strengthens emotional resilience. It reduces fear's influence on the nervous system.

David understood this long before science did. In Psalm 23, he wrote, "He restores my soul." Restoration begins in the inner world. When God restores the soul, He recalibrates thought, memory, perception, and identity. He softens fear's grip by redirecting attention back to His presence. This is why David often spoke to his own mind, saying, "Why are you cast down, O my soul?" He modeled what we now call cognitive reframing, speaking truth to distorted emotion.

The Spirit of God plays a vital role in this renewal. Peace is not something we generate. Peace is something God gives. Jesus said, "My peace I give to you." This peace is not dependent on environment. It does not rise and fall with circumstances. It is internal, spiritual, and supernatural. It defies the patterns that fear creates. It confronts the noise in the mind with a stillness that cannot be explained naturally.

When the Holy Spirit ministers peace, He slows the anxious mind and brings clarity where confusion once ruled. He shifts perspective from danger to presence, from fear to faith. He teaches the believer how to recognize the voice of truth above the voice of panic. He reminds the heart of God's nearness, God's sovereignty, and God's goodness.

This is why prayer is so powerful. Prayer interrupts fear's momentum. It breaks the cycle of anxious rumination. It invites divine presence into the emotional atmosphere. Neuroscience confirms that prayer activates the same regions of the brain associated with focus, calm, and emotional regulation. Prayer does not only move heaven; it also heals the mind.

To experience the mind of Christ is to live from an internal place of order even when external situations are chaotic. It is to possess a peace that regulates emotion before emotion regulates you. Fear loses its authority when the mind is anchored in truth.

The Spirit of peace forms a shield around the heart. The mind of Christ forms clarity within the soul. Together, they create the conditions for healing.

Fear may speak loudly, but peace speaks with authority.

David's Prescription – Worship, Music, and Emotional Healing

David was more than a king and more than a warrior. He was a man who understood the human soul. He knew the weight of fear, the heaviness of sorrow, and the burden of emotional turmoil. Yet he also knew how to return to equilibrium. He cultivated practices that brought his inner world back into alignment. These practices were not accidental. They were intentional tools of survival. In today's language, they would be called emotional regulation strategies.

One of David's greatest gifts was worship. Worship was not entertainment for him. It was therapy. It was medicine. He used music to shift emotional atmosphere and renew internal balance. Scripture records that when Saul was tormented, David played the harp, and relief came. Fear lifted. Oppression broke. Anxiety quieted. The environment changed. This is the essence of what we now call music therapy.

Science affirms the power of sound. Music regulates the nervous system. It lowers cortisol levels. It slows the heart rate. It stabilizes breathing. It activates the parasympathetic system, the part of the body responsible for rest, calm, and restoration. Melodies influence emotions. Rhythm affects the heartbeat. Harmony soothes the mind. David was practicing divine psychology long before the field existed.

His worship was not only outward. It was internal. He used songs to process fear, grief, anger, confusion, and hope. The book of Psalms is the oldest and most honest journal of human emotion ever written. David did not hide what he felt. He confronted it in the presence of God. His words were raw. They were honest. They were unfiltered. He said, "When my heart is overwhelmed, lead me to the rock that is higher than I." This statement reveals a profound understanding of emotional release.

What modern psychologists teach as expressive therapy is what David practiced as worship and journaling. He poured out every emotion before God. He used language to break the pressure of silence. He used song to release the tension stored in the body. He used reflection to reclaim clarity and restore perspective. He never pretended to be strong when he was overwhelmed. He expressed weakness knowing God would turn it into strength.

Worship also has a spiritual effect. It shifts the soul into divine alignment. It opens the heart to the presence of God. It redirects attention from fear to faith, from threat to truth, from emotion to eternity. Worship changes not only how the body feels but how the soul sees. It is a repositioning of perspective. It recalibrates identity. It reminds the heart who God is and who we are in Him.

When David wrote, "Why are you cast down, O my soul?" he was engaging in what psychology calls self-dialogue. He was speaking to his emotions so they would not overpower him. Worship allowed him to separate what he felt from what was true. It allowed him to place truth above fear. Every time he worshiped, he was retraining his mind, releasing his heart, and restoring his equilibrium.

Music and worship reconnected him to God, but they also reconnected him to himself. They grounded him. They slowed him down. They allowed him to breathe again. They created a space where anxiety had no authority and fear had no voice. Many of his psalms begin in distress but end in confidence. The shift did not come from a change in circumstance. It came from a change in internal atmosphere.

David's example teaches us that emotional healing is both spiritual and practical. God uses sound, song, and expression to regulate what fear tries to destabilize. Worship calms the body. It aligns the mind. It strengthens the spirit. It creates room for peace to return.

Fear may rise, but worship rises higher.

The Therapeutic Power of Journaling and Reflection

There are moments when the mind becomes crowded, the heart becomes heavy, and the soul becomes tangled in thoughts that refuse to settle. In such seasons, silence is not strength. Suppression is not discipline. What remains unexpressed begins to accumulate pressure within the body and mind. This is why journaling and reflection are essential tools for healing fear. They create a safe space for what the heart cannot carry alone.

David mastered this discipline long before it was studied in clinical psychology. His psalms are written evidence of a man who refused to let fear stay unspoken. When emotions overwhelmed him, he wrote. When anxiety clouded his mind, he reflected. When sorrow mounted, he poured out his heart in detail. His writings were not polished statements. They were emotional release. They were spiritual processing. They were internal cleansing.

Modern research affirms that expressive writing reduces anxiety, improves mood regulation, lowers stress hormones, and increases clarity of thought. When feelings are transferred from the mind to paper, they lose their power to suffocate. Writing gives fear a place to land so it no longer floats chaotically inside the mind. It is as if the heart exhales through the pen.

Reflection works alongside journaling. Reflection allows the mind to slow down and interpret what has been written. It encourages awareness. It separates emotion from identity. It helps the soul recognize patterns, triggers, and truths that were hidden beneath the surface. Many of David's writings show this shift. He begins with fear, confusion, or distress and ends with confidence, clarity, or worship. The turning point usually happens in the middle through reflection.

Journaling also supports spiritual alignment. When thoughts are written before God, they become prayer. When fears are named, they lose their secrecy. When burdens are expressed, they become petitions. Writing transforms internal chaos into conversation with God. It opens the door for divine reassurance. It makes room for Scripture to speak into specific emotions.

Reflection then invites the mind to evaluate fear through the lens of truth. It redirects attention to God's presence. It creates the mental stillness required to hear His guidance. It brings order where fear brought confusion. It repeats what David modeled when he asked, "Why are you cast down, O my soul?" That question is reflective. It calls the soul back into awareness and alignment.

Journaling and reflection also reveal emotional patterns the body has been holding. They uncover fear that is rooted in past wounds. They expose anxieties that are tied to responsibility, identity, or expectations. They help the believer recognize when the nervous system is overwhelmed. They provide insight into thoughts that need renewing and emotions that need releasing.

These practices do not weaken faith. They strengthen it. A believer who journals is not confessing defeat. They are practicing honesty. A believer who reflects is not overthinking. They are sharpening discernment. God cannot heal what we refuse to acknowledge. Written truth becomes the beginning of inner freedom.

David did not only write when he was in distress. He wrote during victory as well. This pattern teaches another healing principle. Journaling preserves memory. Reflection reinforces gratitude. Both create anchors the heart can return to in future storms. Fear loses authority when we remember how God has delivered us before.

Journaling and reflection are divine invitations to slow down, to listen inward, and to allow truth to reorder what fear has disorganized. They offer the mind relief, the heart expression, and the soul restoration.

Healing flows where expression is allowed.

Rest, Stillness, and the Resetting of the Nervous System

Rest is not weakness. It is not laziness. It is not avoidance. Rest is a spiritual strategy and a biological necessity. When fear overwhelms the body and mind, rest becomes the first medicine. It creates the internal conditions where healing can begin. Stillness is not the absence of movement. It is the intentional slowing of the body and mind so that the soul can hear again.

The nervous system is designed to recover, but only when given space. When fear persists, the body remains in a state of alert. Muscles stay tight. Breathing becomes shallow. The heart works harder. The mind stays vigilant. In this state, peace feels distant because the body has not yet been told that danger is over. Stillness sends that message. It signals safety. It tells the nervous system to reset.

This is why God often begins healing with rest. When Elijah broke under fear, God did not start with correction. He started with sleep. He gave Elijah space to stop, breathe, eat, and recover. Only after the body was calm did God speak. Rest prepares the mind to hear truth. A tired body cannot carry revelation. A restless mind cannot discern direction. Stillness becomes the doorway to restoration.

Science confirms this. Deep breathing activates the parasympathetic system, the part of the nervous system responsible for calm and recovery. Silence reduces cortisol. Slow movement stabilizes heart rhythm. Restful pauses create space in the brain for clarity. The body hears what the mind whispers. When we slow down, we are telling the body that it is safe again.

Scripture affirms this repeatedly. God said, "Be still, and know that I am God." The instruction is physiological and spiritual. Stillness quiets the mind. Stillness grounds the emotions. Stillness allows the heart to remember who God is. It restores identity, perspective, and trust. Stillness does not remove the storm. It removes the storm from the soul.

Rest is also an act of faith. It is the decision to stop striving. It is the choice to trust that God is working even when we are not. It shifts the focus from self-effort to divine presence. In Psalm 23, David said, "He makes me lie down in green pastures." God sometimes leads us into rest because without it we move beyond our emotional capacity. Rest protects the soul from burnout and fear overload.

Stillness invites reflection. Rest invites renewal. Together, they create emotional balance. They slow the racing mind so truth can rise again. They soften the body so the Spirit can minister peace. They open the heart for God to restore what fear has damaged. This is why Jesus often withdrew to lonely places. Not to escape responsibility, but to reset His humanity.

Stillness is not empty. It is purposeful. It is sacred. It is healing.

In a world that celebrates constant movement, rest feels uncomfortable. Yet healing requires it. Fear thrives in noise. Anxiety feeds on activity. Worry multiplies in busyness. Stillness disrupts all of these patterns. It interrupts fear's momentum. It clears emotional fog. It creates space for God's peace to settle.

There are moments when the most spiritual thing you can do is rest. There are battles that are not won through war but through stillness. When the nervous system resets, clarity returns. Strength returns. Perspective returns. Fear loses its grip.

Rest and stillness are not passive. They are powerful tools of healing. They teach the soul to breathe again and remind the heart that God is near.

Peace grows in stillness. Strength rises in rest.

Chapter 10 Reflection

"My flesh and my heart fail;
But God is the strength of my heart and my portion forever."
— Psalm 73:26 (NKJV)

Awareness

Fear often manifests in the body before it forms words. Tension, shallow breathing, fatigue, restlessness, or tightness are not signs of weakness; they are signals.

Where does fear show up in your body first? What physical cues have you learned to ignore or override? When was the last time your body signaled that you were overwhelmed—even if your mind kept pushing forward?

The body remembers what the soul tries to suppress.

Insight

Fear disrupts the body's natural rhythm—sleep, breathing, focus, and emotional regulation. Understanding this removes shame and restores clarity. Some fear responses are biological stress reactions; others are connected to unresolved emotional memory or prolonged pressure.

What thoughts usually accompany your fear? How has fear influenced your decisions by placing your body in constant survival mode?

Fear weakens when it is named rather than resisted.

Alignment

Which truth from this chapter corrects your posture—especially the truth that God is the strength of your heart, not your endurance or effort?

What does it mean for your mind to be "stayed" on God rather than urgency, threat, or control?

"You will keep him in perfect peace,
Whose mind is stayed on You,
Because he trusts in You."
— *Isaiah 26:3 (NKJV)*

Action

Choose **one** practice this week to allow God to reset your mind and body:

- Slow, deep breathing for one minute when tension arises
- Journaling to release internal pressure
- Worship to calm your nervous system
- Stillness without guilt
- Intentional rest as obedience, not escape

Which will you practice consistently?

Declaration

My mind is governed by the peace of God.
My body is not ruled by fear or urgency.
My soul is anchored in divine truth.
I receive the mind of Christ and the rest He provides.
My spirit, soul, and body align with the presence of God.

"He restores my soul."— *Psalm 23:3 (NKJV)*

CHAPTER 11

Fear Is a Spirit

Understanding Its True Nature

Not all fear begins in the mind. Not all fear starts in the body. Some forms of fear arrive quietly, like an unseen visitor, shaping thoughts, influencing emotions, and distorting perception without any physical trigger. Scripture identifies this specific kind of fear as a spirit. Paul was intentional when he wrote, "For God has not given us the spirit of fear." He did not describe it as a feeling or an impulse. He called it a spirit because of its influence, its persistence, and its ability to manipulate the human soul.

Natural responses like caution, alertness, and discernment are part of God's biological and psychological design. These mechanisms help us navigate unfamiliar or threatening environments. Fear is different. Fear disrupts the mind and drains the body. It overwhelms the nervous system. It exaggerates danger and destabilizes peace. It is never protective. It is always depleting. But spiritual fear is even more destructive. It does not begin with the senses. It begins with influence. It does not wait for threat. It creates threat where there is none. It whispers lies, magnifies danger, and attacks the believer's confidence in God.

This chapter is designed to help you discern and defeat fear at its spiritual root. Many people fight emotional fear while unknowingly wrestling against a spiritual influence. They address the symptoms but not the source. They calm the body but ignore the voice speaking into their thoughts. They wage psychological war while overlooking spiritual intrusion. This produces relief but not deliverance.

Paul understood this complexity. He told the church in Ephesus that their battles were not only physical but spiritual. He also reminded the Romans that believers have not received a spirit of bondage that produces fear, but the Spirit of adoption that brings courage and identity. Scripture does not treat fear as a harmless emotion. It treats it as an unwelcome guest that must be recognized and resisted, especially when its origin is spiritual.

Spiritual fear often disguises itself as anxiety, hesitation, or caution. It feels internal, but its origin is external. It attaches itself to emotional wounds, harsh environments, intimidating authority figures, or traumatic memories. It thrives where identity is blurred and truth is not rehearsed. It gains access through stress, negative words, shame, spiritual ignorance, and prolonged emotional exhaustion.

Fear as a spirit manipulates the same neural pathways that emotional fear uses. It plants intrusive thoughts. It reinforces worry through repetition. It magnifies uncertainty until it becomes torment. This is why some forms of fear do not respond to comfort alone. They require spiritual confrontation. They require authority. They require truth spoken boldly. They require alignment with God's presence and God's perspective.

Yet this is not a hopeless battle. What enters spiritually can be defeated spiritually. God has already provided the antidote. He gives power where fear brings weakness. He gives love where fear brings torment. He gives a sound mind where fear produces confusion. Perfect love drives out spiritual fear completely. Divine truth dismantles its lies. Spiritual authority breaks its influence.

This chapter will help you discern the difference between natural fear, emotional fear, and spiritual fear. It will reveal how fear gains access, how it shapes internal narratives, and how to recognize when fear is operating as a spiritual force. It will guide you in resisting its influence, restoring your inner strength, and walking in God's confidence.

Fear may come as an invisible visitor, but it does not have to stay. Once recognized, it can be resisted. Once resisted, it can be silenced. Once silenced, it can be evicted.

Victory begins with discernment.

Understanding Fear Beyond Emotion

Fear is often described as an emotion, but Scripture reveals a deeper dimension. Not every fear comes from memory, experience, or biology. Some fears arrive with no clear trigger. They appear suddenly, persist unnaturally, or intensify beyond logic. These are indicators that fear is functioning beyond emotion. Paul recognized this distinction when he called fear a spirit. He was describing a fear that influences, presses, and distorts, even when circumstances do not support it.

To understand spiritual fear, we must first understand emotional fear. Emotional fear responds to threat. It is the body and mind reacting to uncertainty, pressure, or perceived danger. It has a cause. It follows a pattern. It fades when safety returns. Emotional fear is real, but it is understandable.

Spiritual fear is different. It does not follow natural patterns. It does not respond to reassurance. It does not fade with time. It does not need a reason to exist. It whispers even in peace. It creates panic without cause. It speaks in the voice of the enemy but echoes inside the mind as if it were your own.

Spiritual fear is marked by intrusion. It inserts thoughts that do not belong to the moment. It amplifies insecurity. It revives memories you have already healed from. It creates a heaviness that does not match your environment. It is inconsistent. It is persistent. It is unreasonable. It is fear that does not make sense.

One of the clearest signs of spiritual fear is that it distorts identity. Emotional fear focuses on danger. Spiritual fear focuses on self. It says, you are not enough, you will fail, you are alone, you are unprotected, you are doing something wrong, or you will not make it. These are not emotional reactions. These are spiritual suggestions. They are accusations designed to weaken courage, undermine confidence, and disrupt alignment with God.

Spiritual fear also manipulates perception. A person can be safe and still feel endangered, loved and still feel rejected, provided for and still feel insecure. Spiritual fear alters how life is interpreted. It puts a filter over the mind that makes everything feel threatening. Emotional fear responds to reality. Spiritual fear changes reality.

Spiritual fear is strategic. It often appears during transitions, assignments, ministry, elevation, confrontation, or decision making. It attacks when obedience is required. It intensifies when purpose is awakening. It resists spiritual growth. It functions as an opposing voice, pushing the believer toward retreat rather than advancement.

The psychological parallel to this is intrusive anxiety, intrusive thoughts, and conditioned fear that arrives without context. These experiences show how easily the mind can be influenced. However, spiritual fear goes beyond psychological conditioning. It carries pressure. It carries intimidation. It carries accusation. It carries torment.

Understanding this distinction brings clarity. You cannot counsel away what must be cast out. You cannot ignore what must be confronted. You cannot soothe what must be resisted. Emotional fear needs comfort. Spiritual fear needs authority.

This section lays the foundation for discernment. Before fear can be defeated, it must be recognized. Emotional fear invites self-care. Biological fear invites rest. Spiritual fear invites warfare. Each requires a different response.

Understanding fear beyond emotion helps you reclaim peace, protect your mind, and stand firm in your identity. It opens your eyes to the strategies of the enemy and prepares your heart to walk in the power, love, and soundness that God has already provided.

Fear may begin with a whisper, but once you understand its roots, you silence its influence.

How the Spirit of Fear Gains Access

The spirit of fear does not enter the life of a believer through force. It enters through openings, vulnerabilities, and unguarded places. Scripture often speaks of "doors," "openings," and "gates" because spiritual influences require access points. Fear is no different. Before it becomes a stronghold, it begins as an intrusion that grows through opportunity.

Understanding how fear gains access is essential for breaking its influence. What is not identified cannot be resisted. What is not named cannot be closed.

1. Access Through Trauma and Emotional Shock

Trauma creates cracks in the soul. Sudden loss, betrayal, violence, rejection, or unexpected disruption can overwhelm natural coping mechanisms. In these moments of emotional collapse, fear often enters unchallenged. Trauma does not only wound the heart. It destabilizes identity and disrupts the sense of safety God designed us to live with. Psychologically, trauma heightens the nervous system. Spiritually, trauma weakens defenses. This combination makes the soul vulnerable to spiritual intimidation.

2. Access Through Prolonged Stress and Exhaustion

A tired mind is loud. A tired body is unprotected. Exhaustion breaks emotional stability and weakens discernment. Elijah is a perfect example. His fear did not begin with Jezebel's words. It began with fatigue. Prolonged stress wears down spiritual awareness. The spirit of fear speaks loudly when the soul is drained, frantic, overwhelmed, or overloaded.

Fear often approaches at the end of a long battle, not at the beginning.

3. Access Through Words and Atmospheres

Words create openings. Words spoken by parents, partners, leaders, or authority figures can plant seeds of fear that take root deep in the soul. Statements like "you will fail," "you are not enough," "you cannot handle this," or "something bad is going to happen" carry spiritual weight. When accepted, they become internal narratives that the spirit of fear builds upon.

Environments also matter. Atmospheres filled with conflict, intimidation, manipulation, or negativity weaken inner stability and create spiritual vulnerability.

4. Access Through Generational Patterns

Some fears are learned by observation. Others are inherited through spiritual lineage. Scripture speaks of generational iniquities and familiar spirits, influences that repeat patterns from one generation to another. This is why some families struggle with chronic anxiety, phobias, or cycles of insecurity. Children often internalize the fears of those who raised them, and spiritual fear uses these patterns as open doors.

5. Access Through Shame and Hidden Sin

Shame is one of fear's greatest allies. Shame weakens identity, distorts perception, and convinces the believer that God is distant or displeased. When shame is left unaddressed, it becomes a spiritual entry point. Hidden sin also creates openings, not because God abandons us but because guilt and secrecy weaken spiritual confidence. Fear thrives in secrecy and silence.

6. Access Through Ignorance and Lack of Discernment

Fear gains power where truth is not known. When believers do not understand their authority or their identity, fear takes advantage of the gap. A believer who views fear as normal will tolerate what should be resisted. A believer who does not discern spiritual influence will treat the spirit of fear as a personality trait. Ignorance is not innocence. It is an invitation.

7. Access Through Isolation and Disconnection

Fear grows in isolation. When believers withdraw emotionally, spiritually, or relationally, they become easier targets. Isolation amplifies internal voices and removes the grounding presence that healthy relationships provide. Disconnection from community, from fellowship, or even from self-awareness creates space for fear to speak without interruption.

Fear seeks silence. Faith requires connection.

Recognizing how fear gains access is not meant to create fear. It is meant to create awareness. Awareness empowers. Awareness exposes. Awareness brings clarity. Once these doors are identified, they can be closed. Once the entry points are recognized, they can be sealed. Once the patterns are seen, they can be broken.

The spirit of fear enters through openings, but it cannot stay where truth, authority, and alignment shut the door

The Strategies of the Spirit of Fear

The spirit of fear does not operate randomly. It is strategic, intentional, and calculated. Its goal is not simply to frighten. Its assignment is to weaken, distort, and neutralize. It seeks to sabotage courage, disrupt obedience, and disconnect the believer from spiritual confidence. To defeat fear, one must understand how it functions.

The strategies of this spirit revolve around influence rather than force. It cannot take control unless a believer agrees with its voice. Its power is in persuasion. Its influence is in suggestion. Its strength grows through repetition.

Below are the primary strategies through which the spirit of fear gains dominion.

1. Intimidation Through Imagination

Fear rarely begins with facts. It begins with images. It paints worst-case scenarios. It magnifies small threats. It exaggerates possibilities. It turns imagination into a weapon. This is why fear often feels stronger at night or during moments of vulnerability. It attacks the mind with pictures that feel real. The goal is to erode confidence and replace vision with   dread. This aligns with what psychologists call catastrophic thinking. Fear creates a false future and convinces the mind to react as if it were reality.

2. Whispering Lies Through Internal Dialogue

The spirit of fear speaks in first-person language. It whispers thoughts that sound like your own voice, such as "I cannot handle this," "I am not safe," or "I will fail." These thoughts do not come from you. They come from influence. Fear knows that if it can control the inner dialogue, it can control behavior.

This is why Paul instructed believers to cast down imaginations and every high thing that exalts itself against the knowledge of God. Fear thrives on unchallenged thoughts.

3. Attacking Identity to Weaken Confidence

Fear always targets identity because identity determines courage. When a believer knows who they are, fear loses its power. This is why the spirit of fear often brings accusations. It questions worth, ability, calling, and belonging. It suggests insignificance. It highlights weaknesses. It enlarges failures. It minimizes progress. Fear does not need to stop your assignment. It only needs to convince you that you are not capable of fulfilling it.

4. Amplifying Pressure to Create Panic

The spirit of fear manipulates external pressures and internal expectations. It intensifies deadlines, magnifies demands, and heightens urgency. It creates a sense of "too much" and "not enough" at the same time. This overloads the nervous system and overwhelms the mind.

When pressure feels suffocating, fear is often present. Its strategy is simple. Overload produces paralysis.

5. Using Isolation to Reinforce Vulnerability

Fear thrives when the believer is alone. It grows louder in solitude. It magnifies itself when there is no external voice to challenge its lies. Isolation weakens resistance and strengthens intrusive thoughts. The spirit of fear often pushes people away from support systems, mentors, and community because it knows that truth spoken by others breaks its influence.

Fear seeks silence and secrecy. Faith grows through connection.

6. Creating Cycles of Overthinking and Mental Exhaustion

Overthinking is one of fear's most effective strategies. It traps the mind in loops. It keeps the believer analyzing possibilities without arriving at decision. This drains emotional strength and weakens the ability to trust God. It also interrupts peace, sleep, and clarity. The spirit of fear uses mental exhaustion as an entry point for deeper anxiety.

What psychologists call rumination is often spiritual warfare disguised as overthinking.

7. Mimicking Discernment to Create Confusion

Fear often disguises itself as wisdom. It pretends to be caution. It masquerades as discernment. It sounds like a warning but produces anxiety instead of clarity. True discernment brings peace. Fear brings disturbance. The spirit of fear blurs this line intentionally to make its voice appear reasonable.

Anything that guides you toward confusion is not God.

The spirit of fear does not need a crisis to operate. It only needs agreement. It uses suggestions, images, accusations, and pressures to weaken the heart. Its goal is to break alignment and interrupt confidence.

Once these strategies are exposed, they lose their power. Darkness loses authority when light is present. Fear loses influence when truth is known.

The next section will reveal how to confront and resist the spirit of fear with spiritual authority and divine alignment.

Authority, Identity, and the Power to Resist

The spirit of fear has influence, but it does not have authority. It can suggest, but it cannot enforce. It can intimidate, but it cannot control. Its strength comes from agreement, not power. The moment a believer recognizes their authority and identity in God, fear loses its legal right to operate.

Spiritual authority is not an emotion. It is a position. It is rooted in identity. A believer does not resist fear because they feel confident. They resist fear because they belong to Christ. Authority begins where identity is understood.

1. Identity Breaks Intimidation

Fear thrives where identity is weak. It convinces people they are powerless, inadequate, unprotected, or alone. This is why fear attacked Jesus first with identity. In the wilderness the enemy did not say, you cannot do miracles or you are not anointed. He said, if you are the Son of God. The goal was to shake identity. A shaken identity produces shaken purpose.

The same strategy is used today. The moment a believer remembers who they are, fear begins to collapse.

2. Truth Breaks Agreement

Fear often continues because it has been unchallenged. The moment truth is spoken, agreement is broken. Declaring Scripture out loud is not ritual. It is legal action. It serves spiritual notice. The Word of God dismantles lies, confronts intimidation, and restores sound thinking.

You do not fight fear with silence. You fight fear with truth.

3. Love Breaks Torment

Fear and love cannot occupy the same space. Scripture does not say perfect faith casts out fear. It says perfect love casts out fear. Love brings security. Love brings belonging. Love brings rest. Fear cannot torment where love is embraced. When the believer becomes anchored in the love of God, fear loses its foundation.

Fear does not retreat in the presence of strength. Fear retreats in the presence of love.

4. Authority Breaks Intimidation

Authority is not aggression. It is alignment. It is the believer standing under the Lordship of Christ and speaking from that position. Authority is not the volume of the voice but the certainty of identity.

Jesus did not negotiate with storms, demons, or intimidation. He spoke with clarity. He issued commands. He resisted the enemy with Scripture.

Authority is exercised, not internalized. You do not think authority. You speak it.

5. Resistance Breaks Momentum

Fear gains power when tolerated. It weakens when resisted. Scripture says resist the devil and he will flee. The word flee does not mean walk away slowly. It means run in panic. The spirit of fear cannot endure sustained resistance. Every time the believer refuses agreement, fear loses strength.

Consistency is more important than intensity. One consistent no weakens fear more than one emotional prayer.

6. Action Breaks Paralysis

Fear's final goal is stagnation. It wants to stop movement. It wants to block obedience. It wants to prevent advancement. The antidote is simple. Movement. The moment a believer acts in the direction of God's will, even trembling, fear is defeated. Authority becomes visible through action.

God does not require the absence of fear for obedience. He requires alignment.

Authority, identity, truth, love, resistance, and action form the spiritual framework for breaking the influence of fear. Together they rebuild the inner foundation that the enemy attempts to erode.

A believer who knows their identity becomes unshakeable. A believer who speaks truth becomes unstoppable. A believer who rests in love becomes untouchable.

When identity is settled and authority is exercised, fear no longer dictates decisions. The spirit of fear can knock, but it cannot enter. It can speak, but it cannot persuade. It can threaten, but it cannot control.

The presence of fear is not failure. Agreement with fear is defeat. Resistance to fear is victory.

Every believer will encounter fear at emotional, biological, and spiritual levels, but fear is never the final authority. The spirit of fear can intimidate, but it cannot override divine identity. Its influence ends where truth is enforced, where authority is exercised, and where the believer refuses agreement. The presence of fear is not the evidence of weakness. Agreement with fear is the only defeat. When the soul stands firm in identity, speaks truth with confidence, and resists intimidation with spiritual authority, fear loses its grip and flees.

War against fear is won through discernment and alignment. Discernment exposes the lie. Identity confronts intimidation. Authority dismantles influence. Resistance breaks momentum. There is nothing passive about freedom. It is the active choice to reject fear and return to the truth of who God is and who we are in Him.

Yet, spiritual warfare is not the final destination of healing. God has provided something greater than resistance, greater than courage, greater than authority. Fear does not leave simply because we fight hard enough. Fear leaves because something stronger takes its place. Its ultimate defeat is not found in power or discipline. Its final expulsion comes from security.

The next chapter will reveal the ultimate cure that Scripture presents for spiritual fear: perfect love and Divine perspectives about fear.

Chapter 11 Reflection

Fear Is a Spirit — Understanding Its True Nature

Anchor Scripture

"For God has not given us a spirit of fear, but of power and of love and of a sound mind."
— 2 Timothy 1:7 (NKJV)

Awareness

Some fear does not originate from circumstance, memory, or physical threat. It arrives without warning, lingers without logic, and presses without relief.

Where have you experienced fear that did not match your situation—fear that felt intrusive, persistent, or disproportionate? What thoughts repeatedly surface without invitation? In what moments does fear feel imposed rather than reactive?

Discernment begins when you recognize that not all fear is emotional.

Insight

This chapter reveals that fear can operate as a spiritual influence—suggesting lies, distorting identity, and magnifying threat without evidence. Unlike emotional fear, spiritual fear does not fade with reassurance. It thrives on agreement and repetition.

What did you recognize about how fear speaks—through imagination, internal dialogue, accusation, pressure, or overthinking? How has fear attempted to weaken your confidence, obedience, or sense of safety by targeting your identity rather than your environment?

Fear gains strength through agreement, not authority.

Alignment

Which truth from this chapter corrects your response to fear—especially the truth that fear is not from God and therefore does not have permission to govern your mind?

Where do you need to realign with your identity as a child of God—adopted, protected, and empowered rather than intimidated or uncertain?

"You did not receive the spirit of bondage again to fear, but you received the Spirit of adoption..."
— *Romans 8:15 (NKJV)*

Action

Identify **one area** where you will actively resist agreement with fear this week:

- Speaking Scripture aloud when fear intrudes
- Challenging internal accusations with truth
- Refusing isolation and choosing connection
- Acting in obedience even when fear speaks

What practical step will you take to exercise authority rather than tolerate intimidation?

Declaration

"Fear is not my master and intimidation is not my guide. I have not received a spirit of fear, but of power, love, and a sound mind.

I reject every lie that attacks my identity or weakens my confidence.I stand in truth, I walk in authority, and I remain anchored in God's love.

Fear has no agreement with me, and therefore no influence over me."

CHAPTER 12

Perfect Love Casts Out Fear

Living with Divine Perspectives

Anytime you are combating a spiritual issue at any level, the easiest way to engage victoriously is to see through divine perspectives. Fear loses power when the believer stops interpreting life through emotion and begins to interpret life through the eyes of God. Divine perspective aligns the soul with truth. It positions the heart to respond from victory rather than survival.

God was the first to address the problem of fear, long before humanity understood the extent of its damage. He knew that fear is one of the most strategic weapons the enemy uses to cage destiny, interrupt purpose, delay obedience, and alter the course of His agenda in the life of an individual, a family, a nation, or a generation. Fear is subtle. It does not always roar. Sometimes it whispers. It creeps in quietly and shapes decisions without announcing itself. For that reason God never waited for people to recognize fear before He provided an antidote.

From Genesis to Revelation, God consistently confronted fear before commissioning people into purpose. When Abraham trembled at the uncertainty of the future, God did not give strategy first. He gave security. In a vision He said, "Do not be afraid, Abram. I am your shield, your very great reward." God did not remove uncertainty. He removed fear. God was teaching that the antidote to fear is not more information but deeper assurance.

When Joshua was appointed to lead a nation into battle and into territory takeover, to possess what God had promised their ancestor by covenant, God did not begin with military training, strategic planning, or leadership theory. He began by addressing the anticipatory problem of fear. "Be strong and courageous, do not be afraid." God administered a preventive prescription before the assignment even began. Before Joshua faced giants, God fought for his confidence. Before Joshua held a sword, God handed him truth. The message was clear. The greatest threat to destiny is not always an external enemy but internal intimidation. Fear neutralizes leadership long before warfare begins.

Even Jesus approached fear through divine perspective. In Gethsemane His soul grew sorrowful to the point of death, yet His emotional anguish never translated into fear. He felt deeply, yet He did not retreat. His emotions were present, but they did not regulate His obedience. He framed Gethsemane through the Father's will instead of through human distress. His example teaches that emotional pain does not automatically mean fear is present. Divine perspective is what keeps the soul steady.

This chapter explores God's antidote to fear. Scripture reveals two dimensions of victory. One is preventive. The other is corrective. There is the posture that keeps fear from entering, and there is the weapon that expels fear once it has already entered. Both are rooted in the same source: perfect love.

Perfect love is not flawless emotion. It is complete security. It is the deep assurance that God is present, God is committed, God is dependable, God is protective, and God is eternally for you. Perfect love uproots fear because fear cannot coexist where the soul is anchored in belonging. Fear is weakened by warfare, but fear is expelled by love.

This chapter is not about trying to confront fear harder. It is about discovering the realm where fear no longer has a legal right to stay.

Divine Perspective — How God Sees Fear

To defeat fear, we must first understand how God sees it. Spiritual victory begins not with reaction but with perspective. Most people confront fear from the inside out, beginning with emotion and trying to fight their way toward truth. God confronts fear from the opposite direction. He starts with truth and brings the heart into alignment. Divine perspective reframes fear before fear has an opportunity to shape interpretation.

Fear looks overwhelming when viewed from the human lens. It feels powerful because it operates through emotion, memory, imagination, and the nervous system. But from God's viewpoint, fear is not a force to coexist with or manage. It is an intruder. It is a lie. It is an unauthorized voice attempting to occupy a place in the soul that God never assigned to it.

This is why God never spoke casually around fear. He confronted it directly every time it appeared. He did not negotiate with it. He did not normalize it. He did not tell His people to learn to live with it. When fear surfaced, God silenced it. He said, do not be afraid. He said, fear not. He said, be strong and courageous. These were not motivational slogans. They were divine decrees revealing how God sees fear.

This perspective corrects a common cultural message that has become popular: "do it afraid." There are believers who have been taught to obey God while allowing fear to remain in the soul. Many have repeated this message because it sounds practical and relatable. But when dealing with the spirit of fear, this advice is spiritually dangerous. The spirit of fear cannot be tolerated, accommodated, or cohabited with. It will always antagonize the will of God. It does not retreat if given space. It grows. It waits for moments of vulnerability. It attacks identity, resists obedience, and distorts perception. The enemy does not want you simply to be afraid. He wants fear to become the lens through which you interpret God.

The Bible does not teach "do it afraid." The Bible teaches "do not be afraid." God's method is zero tolerance, and His language reveals His posture toward fear. To Abraham, He said, do not be afraid. To Isaac, do not be afraid. To Jacob, do not be afraid. To Moses, do not be afraid. To Joshua, He commanded, be strong and courageous. To David, He revealed, the Lord is my light and salvation, whom shall I fear. To Mary, do not be afraid. To Joseph, do not be afraid. To Paul, do not be afraid, for I am with you. Many of the messages God sent through Isaiah began with the same command because fear was not viewed as a personality trait but as a spiritual threat. Fear not was never a gentle encouragement. It was a divine boundary line drawn around the soul.

Divine perspective teaches that fear is not a sign of humility. It is a sign of misplaced focus. God was not telling Joshua to suppress emotion. He was instructing him to shift attention. Courage is not the absence of feeling. Courage is the presence of the right focus. Fear grows when the mind magnifies threat. Courage grows when the mind magnifies God.

When you begin to see fear the way God sees it, you realize that fear is not destiny. It is not identity. It is not a reasonable companion. It is an intruder that must be confronted. God does not require believers to pretend they do not feel fear. He requires them to refuse partnership with the voice of fear.

From God's perspective, fear interrupts peace, clarity, obedience, and alignment. Every time God says do not be afraid, He is not reprimanding emotion. He is inviting the soul into security and belonging. Divine perspective protects the believer from allowing emotion to become agreement.

Victory over fear does not start with trying harder. It starts with seeing clearer. When fear is viewed the way heaven views it, its influence is dismantled before the battle even begins.

The Preventive Cure — How Perfect Love Keeps Fear Out

Deliverance from fear does not begin with confrontation. It begins with prevention. Scripture teaches that fear can be expelled, but it also teaches that fear can be kept out altogether. God does not only provide treatment for fear. He provides immunity. That immunity is called perfect love.

Perfect love is often misunderstood. Many assume it refers to flawless affection or intense emotion. Biblically, perfect love means complete security. It is the deep assurance that God is present, committed, protective, and permanently for you. It is love without instability. It is belonging that cannot be revoked. This kind of love becomes insulation against fear because fear thrives where security is absent.

Fear survives on uncertainty. It feeds on doubt, rejection, insecurity, emotional neglect, instability, and perceived danger. Fear cannot thrive where the soul is anchored in the certainty of God's love. This is why Scripture says perfect love casts out fear. Fear does not leave because you fight harder. Fear leaves when the heart becomes convinced that it is safe.

The original Greek word translated as fear in 1 John 4:18 is phobos. In this verse it does not refer to ordinary caution or emotional alarm. It refers to tormenting fear, the kind that expects punishment, abandonment, or rejection. John was addressing believers whose emotional and spiritual security had been shaken. They were afraid of judgment and afraid that their weaknesses disqualified them from God. This is why he said fear has torment. The word torment in Greek, kolasis, literally means the anticipation of punishment. John was teaching that fear remains wherever love is not yet believed. Perfect love does not simply comfort fear. It removes the foundation fear stands on by convincing the soul that it is safe in God.

Perfect love keeps fear out in three ways:

1. **Perfect love establishes identity.** Fear finds entry where identity is unstable. When you know you are loved, chosen, protected, and backed by God, you stop interpreting life as if you were alone.

2. **Perfect love establishes belonging.** Fear convinces people that they must perform to be accepted or succeed to be valuable. Perfect love provides safety without performance. You are loved because you belong, not because you never fail.

3. **Perfect love establishes trust.** Fear questions the future. Perfect love settles the future before it arrives. It reassures the heart that God will be God in every season.

God did not begin Joshua's journey by addressing strategy. He began by securing identity and belonging. Joshua needed to know that he was never alone, never unsupported, and never unprotected. Before entering war, he had to be established in love.

Perfect love is preventive. It protects the soul before fear has a chance to build arguments. When the believer is rooted in perfect love, fear loses its voice because it has nothing left to negotiate with. Threat does not equal danger. Delay does not equal abandonment. Correction does not equal rejection. Transition does not equal instability. Failure does not equal identity loss.

The goal is not to become fearless. The goal is to become anchored. When the soul rests in the certainty of God's character, fear can knock but it cannot stay. Perfect love is not the avoidance of difficulty. It is the assurance that nothing in life or death, success or failure, comfort or pressure, can separate you from God's intention and affection.

Perfect love is not a feeling you wait for. It is a truth you root yourself in. It is a position you stand in. It is a lens you think through. The more the heart becomes grounded in this reality, the less room fear has to function. Where perfect love is practiced, fear loses permission to stay.

The Corrective Cure — How Truth Expels Fear Once It Has Entered

Even the strongest believers can experience moments when fear slips in. Fear does not always enter with crisis. Sometimes it enters through disappointment, exhaustion, uncertainty, delay, guilt, shame, self-doubt, or painful memories. Perfect love prevents fear from entering, but when fear has already taken root, truth becomes the corrective cure.

Fear cannot remain where truth is revealed and believed. Fear survives on illusion, exaggeration, imagination, and distortion. It magnifies what is temporary and hides what is eternal. Fear does not need facts to operate. It only needs agreement. Once the believer agrees with the voice of fear, fear becomes a false teacher and a false prophet in the soul.

This is why the corrective cure for fear is not denial, emotional strength, or self-reassurance. The corrective cure is truth. Jesus said you will know the truth and the truth will make you free. Truth is not information. Truth is revelation that confronts lies. Fear loses power when the lie behind it is exposed.

There are three primary lies that fuel fear in the hearts of believers:

1. **The lie of abandonment.** The belief that God is distant, indifferent, or uninvolved.

2. **The lie of inadequacy.** The belief that who I am or what I have is not enough.

3. **The lie of danger without protection.** The belief that what threatens me is stronger than the God who surrounds me.

Fear grows in the areas where these lies remain unchallenged. The moment truth confronts the lie, fear begins to wither. For example:

- The lie of abandonment is destroyed by the truth, I will never leave you nor forsake you.

- The lie of inadequacy is destroyed by the truth, My grace is sufficient for you.

- The lie of danger without protection is destroyed by the truth, He will give His angels charge over you to keep you in all your ways.

Truth does not ignore reality. Truth interprets reality through God. David did not defeat fear by acting as if danger did not exist. He defeated fear by declaring, The Lord is my light and my salvation, whom shall I fear. He did not say there was nothing to fear. He said there was Someone greater than fear.

Truth does not silence emotion. Truth regulates emotion. When truth becomes internalized, fear loses the ability to dominate decision making. This is why Scripture repeatedly instructs believers to meditate, remember, declare, write, sing, and call to mind. These are not religious rituals. They are spiritual technologies that uproot the lies that fear builds.

The corrective cure for fear requires participation. Fear may leave suddenly, but most often fear leaves progressively through renewed thinking. Paul described this process when he said, be transformed by the renewing of your mind. Truth rewires perception until the soul stops agreeing with fear.

Fear cannot be cast out by force while the lie that empowers it remains untouched. A believer can command fear to leave and still feel fear later if the lie inside was not replaced by truth. This is why God works gently with His people. He exposes lies, reveals truth, and strengthens the believer until confidence in God becomes louder than intimidation.

Where truth is embraced, fear loses oxygen. It cannot survive in a soul that is convinced of God's nature, God's nearness, and God's commitment.

When the preventive cure of perfect love and the corrective cure of truth operate together, fear has no legal right to influence the mind, emotions, or identity.

The Weapon of Alignment — Living Permanently Fear-Free

Permanent victory over fear is not accidental. It is the result of alignment. Fear loses power not only when love is received and truth is embraced, but when the believer chooses to live from the posture God designed. Alignment is the intentional positioning of the heart under the government of God. It is living in agreement with His Word, His character, and His perspective.

Many believers conquer fear temporarily but later experience a relapse because they return to old patterns of thinking. They receive comfort in crisis, but once peace returns, they stop practicing the habits that regulate their soul. Alignment is what turns temporary relief into permanent stability. It is not a one-time victory. It is a lifestyle rooted in daily agreement with God.

Alignment has three pillars:

1. **Agreement with identity.** Fear grows when the believer forgets who they are. Alignment begins with remembering that you are loved, chosen, seen, protected, empowered, and backed by God. Identity is your spiritual address. Wherever identity is stable, fear has no entry point.

2. **Agreement with truth.** Truth is not a moment of revelation. It is a continuous practice. Alignment means choosing truth again and again, especially when emotions attempt to negotiate another narrative. Thoughts are not neutral.

Agreement determines direction. The soul follows whatever it consistently agrees with.

3. **Agreement with presence.** Alignment becomes effortless when the heart is aware of God's nearness. Fear relies on the illusion of abandonment. Alignment is the daily awareness that God is here, God is involved, God is watching, God is guiding, and God is for me.

Alignment does not prevent storms, but it prevents fear from dominating in storms. Jesus slept in a storm not because He was numb to danger, but because He was aligned with the Father. Alignment does not remove pressure, but it removes intimidation. Alignment does not avoid responsibility, but it removes the torment attached to responsibility.

When fear tries to return, alignment responds quickly and confidently:

- Fear says you are alone Alignment says God is with me
- Fear says you are not enough Alignment says His grace is sufficient
- Fear says danger is greater than protection Alignment says The Lord is my shield

Living fear-free does not mean living emotion-free. It means emotion is not the regulator of decisions. The heart may feel pressure, but the spirit remains steady because alignment keeps God, not fear, at the center.

Alignment becomes a weapon when it is practiced daily.

- Choosing worship over worry
- Choosing Scripture over speculation
- Choosing declarations over rumination
- Choosing gratitude over catastrophizing

- Choosing rest over emotional exhaustion

These are not random choices. They are acts of spiritual warfare. Each one reinforces perfect love and truth in the soul and limits fear's access.

The believer who remains aligned does not merely recover from fear. They become unshakable. Peace becomes their default state, not a temporary condition. Courage becomes natural because confidence is anchored. Even when new situations arise, fear does not regain dominance because alignment has closed the door it once entered through.

Alignment builds the kind of inner strength that does not need conditions to be perfect in order to remain at peace. It trains the soul to live from belonging, not survival. It is the daily choice to think, speak, decide, and interpret from God's perspective.

Where alignment is practiced, fear does not return.

Chapter 12 Reflection

> *"There is no fear in love; but perfect love casts out fear, because fear involves torment."*
> *— 1 John 4:18 (NKJV)*

Awareness

Where has fear been influencing your thoughts, decisions, or emotional responses—especially in subtle ways that feel normal or justified? Identify the areas where fear has quietly shaped your sense of safety, worth, or belonging.

Insight

What did this chapter reveal about fear's ultimate weakness—that fear loses its power where love is received, not earned? How has misunderstanding God's love allowed fear to remain active in your life?

Alignment

Which truth about God's love corrects your internal narrative—especially the belief that safety, acceptance, or peace must be achieved through control, performance, or self-protection?

Action

What intentional step will you take to practice resting in God's love this week—through stillness, prayer, Scripture meditation, or choosing trust over fear in a specific situation?

Declaration

I am fully loved and completely secure in God.

Perfect love governs my thoughts, steadies my emotions, and anchors my identity.

Fear no longer has authority over me.

I live from love, move in peace, and walk in freedom.

CHAPTER 13

CONCLUSION

PRESCRIPTION FOR FEAR

Thank you for reading *Rx for Fear*. I hope you have been enlightened. My goal has been to provide an evidence-based solution to the harassment and torment of fear. This conclusion presents the actual prescription that consistently works.

The dosage is as needed and has no limit. The only condition is alignment with the only One who has authority over fear. There is a Spirit that He alone can give. For the spirit of fear to be silenced, you must align with Him for the Spirit of love, the Spirit of power, and the Spirit of a sound mind.

Below are the categories of fear and the prescription you need.

CATEGORY 1

Fear Rooted in the Past

Triggers:

Secrets, guilt, shame, trauma, painful memories, consequences, exposure

Emotional Symptoms:

Regret, self-condemnation, replaying the past, low self-esteem, self-sabotage, perfectionism, difficulty receiving love, unworthiness

Physical Symptoms:

Tension headaches, fatigue after emotional memories, sleep disturbance, nightmares, digestive discomfort

Biblical Character:

Peter after denying Jesus (John 18; John 21)

Scripture:

1. As far as the east is from the west, so far has He removed our transgressions from us. Psalm 103:12

2. I—yes, I alone—will blot out your sins for my own sake and will never think of them again. Isaiah 43:25

3. If we confess our sins, He is faithful and just to forgive us our sins and to cleanse us from all unrighteousness. 1 John 1:9

4. Let us draw near with a true heart in full assurance of faith, having our hearts sprinkled from an evil conscience. Hebrews 10:22

5. Therefore, if anyone is in Christ, he is a new creation; old things have passed away; behold, all things have become new. 2 Corinthians 5:17

6. There is therefore now no condemnation to those who are in Christ Jesus. Romans 8:1

7. Confess your trespasses to one another, and pray for one another, that you may be healed. James 5:16

8. He who covers his sins will not prosper, but whoever confesses and forsakes them will have mercy. Proverbs 28:13

9. Have mercy upon me, O God, according to Your lovingkindness; according to the multitude of Your tender mercies, blot out my transgressions. Psalm 51:1

10. Therefore, having been justified by faith, we have peace with God through our Lord Jesus Christ. Romans 5:1

11. For I will be merciful to their unrighteousness, and their sins and their lawless deeds I will remember no more. Hebrews 8:12

Prayer:

Father, thank You that my past is not my prison. I confess my sins and receive Your forgiveness and cleansing. I release shame, guilt, and every memory trying to define me. I am a new creation and there is no condemnation for me in Christ Jesus. Heal every place wounded by my past and let mercy rewrite my story. Amen.

CATEGORY 2

Fear Concerning the Present

Triggers:

Needs not met, financial stress, danger, sickness, uncertainty, addiction and dependency

Emotional Symptoms:

Anxiety, restlessness, irritability, indecision, unhealthy coping, overwhelm

Physical Symptoms:

Racing heartbeat, muscle tension, panic attacks, shortness of breath, cravings or withdrawals, sleep disruption

Biblical Character:

The Widow of Zarephath (1 Kings 17:12)

Scripture:

1. God is our refuge and strength, a very present help in trouble. Psalm 46:1

2. Take therefore no thought, saying, What shall we eat? or, What shall we drink? or, Wherewithal shall we be clothed? (For after all these things do the Gentiles seek:) for your heavenly Father knoweth that ye have need of all these things. Matthew 6:31–32

3. Casting all your care upon him; for he careth for you. 1 Peter 5:7

4. When thou passest through the waters, I will be with thee; and through the rivers, they shall not overflow thee: when thou

walkest through the fire, thou shalt not be burned; neither shall the flame kindle upon thee. Isaiah 43:2

5. These things I have spoken unto you, that in me ye might have peace. In the world ye shall have tribulation: but be of good cheer; I have overcome the world. John 16:33

6. Peace I leave with you, my peace I give unto you: not as the world giveth, give I unto you. Let not your heart be troubled, neither let it be afraid. John 14:27

7. I have been young, and now am old; yet have I not seen the righteous forsaken, nor his seed begging bread. Psalm 37:25

8. The eternal God is thy refuge, and underneath are the everlasting arms: and he shall thrust out the enemy from before thee; and shall say, Destroy them. Deuteronomy 33:27

9. He shall deliver thee in six troubles: yea, in seven there shall no evil touch thee. Job 5:19

10. Teaching them to observe all things whatsoever I have commanded you: and, lo, I am with you alway, even unto the end of the world. Amen. Matthew 28:20

11. The Lord is my shepherd; I shall not want. Psalm 23:1

12. But he was wounded for our transgressions, he was bruised for our iniquities: the chastisement of our peace was upon him; and with his stripes we are healed. Isaiah 53:5

13. But my God shall supply all your need according to his riches in glory by Christ Jesus. Philippians 4:19

14. Be careful for nothing; but in every thing by prayer and supplication with thanksgiving let your requests be made known unto God. And the peace of God, which passeth all understanding, shall keep your hearts and minds through Christ Jesus. Philippians 4:6–7

15. Come unto me, all ye that labour and are heavy laden, and I will give you rest. Matthew 11:28

16. There hath no temptation taken you but such as is common to man: but God is faithful, who will not suffer you to be tempted above that ye are able; but will with the temptation also make a way to escape, that ye may be able to bear it. 1 Corinthians 10:13

17. God is in the midst of her; she shall not be moved: God shall help her, and that right early. Psalm 46:5

18. And be not drunk with wine, wherein is excess; but be filled with the Spirit. Ephesians 5:18

19. All things are lawful unto me, but all things are not expedient: all things are lawful for me, but I will not be brought under the power of any. 1 Corinthians 6:12

Prayer:

Lord, You are my Shepherd and my present help. Break every dependency fueled by fear. I cast every care on You. You supply every need. I refuse anxiety. Sin shall not have dominion over me. I receive Your strength and rest today. Amen.

Declaration:

I am not ruled by cravings or cycles.

I am filled with the Spirit and controlled by nothing else.

Sin shall not have dominion over me.

Every chain is broken.

I walk in liberty, strength, and soundness of mind.

I am free, and I remain free.

CATEGORY 3

Fear Concerning the Future

Triggers:

Prophecies, unknown outcomes, aging, death, change, disappointments

Biblical Character:

Joshua (Joshua 1)

Scripture:

1. For I know the thoughts that I think toward you, saith the Lord, thoughts of peace, and not of evil, to give you an expected end. Jeremiah 29:11

2. Have not I commanded thee? Be strong and of a good courage; be not afraid, neither be thou dismayed: for the Lord thy God is with thee whithersoever thou goest. Joshua 1:9

3. Take therefore no thought for the morrow: for the morrow shall take thought for the things of itself. Sufficient unto the day is the evil thereof. Matthew 6:34

4. And why take ye thought for raiment? Consider the lilies of the field, how they grow; they toil not, neither do they spin: And yet I say unto you, That even Solomon in all his glory was not arrayed like one of these. Wherefore, if God so clothe the grass of the field, which to day is, and to morrow is cast into the oven, shall he not much more clothe you, O ye of little faith? Matthew 6:28–30

Prayer:

Father, You hold my tomorrow. Redirect my fear into hope and turn unpredictability into expectation. Amen.

CATEGORY 4

Fear in Relationships

Triggers:

Disapproval, abandonment, rejection, betrayal, criticism, loneliness

Biblical Character:

Hagar (Genesis 16; 21)

Scripture:

1. When my father and my mother forsake me, then the Lord will take me up. Psalm 27:10

2. Let your conversation be without covetousness; and be content with such things as ye have: for he hath said, I will never leave thee, nor forsake thee. Hebrews 13:5

3. But now thus saith the Lord that created thee, O Jacob, and he that formed thee, O Israel, Fear not: for I have redeemed thee, I have called thee by thy name; thou art mine. Isaiah 43:1

4. Can a woman forget her sucking child, that she should not have compassion on the son of her womb? yea, they may forget, yet will I not forget thee. Behold, I have graven thee upon the palms of my hands; thy walls are continually before me. Isaiah 49:15–16

5. The Lord hath appeared of old unto me, saying, Yea, I have loved thee with an everlasting love: therefore with lovingkindness have I drawn thee. Jeremiah 31:3

Prayer:

Lord, heal every wound of rejection and abandonment. Establish my identity in Your perfect love. Amen.

CATEGORY 5

Fear in Personal Growth and Destiny

Triggers:

Success, visibility, purpose, assignment, new levels, responsibility

Biblical Character:

Moses (Exodus 3–4)

Scripture:

1. And he said, My presence shall go with thee, and I will give thee rest. Exodus 33:14

2. For God hath not given us the spirit of fear; but of power, and of love, and of a sound mind. 2 Timothy 1:7

3. I can do all things through Christ which strengtheneth me. Philippians 4:13

4. For by thee I have run through a troop; and by my God have I leaped over a wall. Psalm 18:29

5. Then he answered and spake unto me, saying, This is the word of the Lord unto Zerubbabel, saying, Not by might, nor by power, but by my spirit, saith the Lord of hosts. Zechariah 4:6

6. Fear thou not; for I am with thee: be not dismayed; for I am thy God: I will strengthen thee; yea, I will help thee; yea, I will uphold thee with the right hand of my righteousness. Isaiah 41:10

7. For they got not the land in possession by their own sword, neither did their own arm save them: but thy right hand, and thine arm, and the light of thy countenance, because thou hadst a favour unto them. Psalm 44:3

8. Who art thou, O great mountain? before Zerubbabel thou shalt become a plain: and he shall bring forth the headstone thereof with shoutings, crying, Grace, grace unto it. Zechariah 4:7

9. I have more understanding than all my teachers: for thy testimonies are my meditation. Psalm 119:99

Prayer:

Lord, I refuse to shrink from destiny. You strengthen me and uphold me. Every mountain becomes a plain. I step boldly into everything You prepared for me. Amen.

CATEGORY 6

Fear from External Threats

Triggers:

Disaster, violence, war, danger, hostility, insecurity

Biblical Character:

Jehoshaphat (2 Chronicles 20)

Scripture:

Thou shalt not be afraid for the terror by night; nor for the arrow that flieth by day. Psalm 91:5

Therefore will not we fear, though the earth be removed, and though the mountains be carried into the midst of the sea. Psalm 46:2

Behold, they shall surely gather together, but not by me: whosoever shall gather together against thee shall fall for thy sake. Isaiah 54:15

So shall they fear the name of the Lord from the west, and his glory from the rising of the sun. When the enemy shall come in like a flood, the Spirit of the Lord shall lift up a standard against him. Isaiah 59:19

Associate yourselves, O ye people, and ye shall be broken in pieces; and give ear, all ye of far countries: gird yourselves, and ye shall be broken in pieces; gird yourselves, and ye shall be broken in pieces. Take counsel together, and it shall come to nought; speak the word, and it shall not stand: for God is with us. Isaiah 8:9–10

The Lord shall cause thine enemies that rise up against thee to be smitten before thy face: they shall come out against thee one way, and flee before thee seven ways. Deuteronomy 28:7

Behold, I give unto you power to tread on serpents and scorpions, and over all the power of the enemy: and nothing shall by any means hurt you. Luke 10:19

In righteousness shalt thou be established: thou shalt be far from oppression; for thou shalt not fear: and from terror; for it shall not come near thee. Isaiah 54:14

Prayer:

Lord, You are my refuge and defense. Every gathering against me falls. I am established in righteousness and far from oppression. Nothing shall by any means hurt me. Amen.

CATEGORY 7

Fear of Identity and Self

Triggers:

Inadequacy, insignificance, comparison, irrelevance, wasted years

Biblical Character:

Gideon (Judges 6)

Scripture:

1. Fear thou not; for I am with thee: be not dismayed; for I am thy God: I will strengthen thee; yea, I will help thee; yea, I will uphold thee with the right hand of my righteousness. Isaiah 41:10

2. I will praise thee; for I am fearfully and wonderfully made: marvellous are thy works; and that my soul knoweth right well. Psalm 139:14

3. But by the grace of God I am what I am: and his grace which was bestowed upon me was not in vain; but I laboured more abundantly than they all: yet not I, but the grace of God which was with me. 1 Corinthians 15:10

4. But ye are a chosen generation, a royal priesthood, an holy nation, a peculiar people; that ye should shew forth the praises of him who hath called you out of darkness into his marvellous light. 1 Peter 2:9

5. Thou shalt no more be termed Forsaken; neither shall thy land any more be termed Desolate: but thou shalt be called Hephzibah, and thy land Beulah: for the Lord delighteth in thee, and thy land shall be married. Isaiah 62:4

6. Before I formed thee in the belly I knew thee; and before thou camest forth out of the womb I sanctified thee, and I ordained thee a prophet unto the nations. Jeremiah 1:5

7. And he said unto me, My grace is sufficient for thee: for my strength is made perfect in weakness. Most gladly therefore will I rather glory in my infirmities, that the power of Christ may rest upon me. 2 Corinthians 12:9

8. For we are his workmanship, created in Christ Jesus unto good works, which God hath before ordained that we should walk in them. Ephesians 2:10

9. Being confident of this very thing, that he which hath begun a good work in you will perform it until the day of Jesus Christ. Philippians 1:6

10. And I will restore to you the years that the locust hath eaten, the cankerworm, and the caterpiller, and the palmerworm, my great army which I sent among you. Joel 2:25

Prayer:

Father, thank You that I am who You say I am. I am chosen, known, loved, and complete in You. Let truth silence every lie. My identity is secure. Amen.

QUICK REFERENCE

Tangible Strategies for Overcoming Fear

SUMMARY OF STRATEGIES DEMONSTRATED

- Honest conversation with God
- Returning to purpose
- Accepting help
- Identity reset in God's presence
- Journaling and writing
- Remembering past victories
- Worship and music
- Prophetic self-talk
- Physical and emotional renewal
- Community and fasting
- Gratitude-based prayer
- Scriptural reframing
- Staying connected
- Learning from mistakes
- Taking action while afraid

FINAL NOTE

Fear is not driven out by willpower. It departs by alignment. When the Spirit of love, the Spirit of power, and the Spirit of a sound mind fill the heart, fear loses its legal right to remain.

This prescription has no limit and no side effects. Take as needed until every part of your life is governed by peace.

You are loved.
You are protected.
You are strengthened.
You are safe in God.

You will win this battle.
You are already healed from fear.
And you will never live under the torment of fear again.

⬤ CONTRAINDICATION: MISALIGNMENT WITH TRUTH

This prescription functions **only in alignment**. Scripture is clear: authority, peace, and protection are **not activated** where rebellion, unrepented sin, or willful disobedience are tolerated. Fear entered humanity through disobedience, and it continues to thrive where sin is concealed rather than confronted. Outward composure cannot silence inward guilt. For this prescription to work, it must be taken with **faith, repentance, obedience, fellowship, and truth**.

> "Say to the righteous that it shall be well with them,
> For they shall eat the fruit of their doings.
> Woe to the wicked! It shall be ill with him,
> For the reward of his hands shall be given him."
> *(Isaiah 3:10–11, NKJV)*

> "Shall we continue in sin that grace may abound? Certainly not!"
> *(Romans 6:1–2, NKJV)*

> "Who may ascend into the hill of the Lord?
> Or who may stand in His holy place?
> He who has clean hands and a pure heart."
> *(Psalm 24:3–4, NKJV)*

> "If I regard iniquity in my heart,
> The Lord will not hear."
> *(Psalm 66:18, NKJV)*

Alignment is not punishment. It is **protection**.
Conviction is not condemnation. It is **correction**.
Repentance is not loss. It is **restoration**.

ONE-PAGE PRESCRIPTION FOR FEAR
A Scriptural Alignment Guide for Daily Victory

Fear is not resolved by analysis.
Fear yields to truth consistently applied.

FEAR IS NOT MY PORTION

The Lord is my light and my salvation; therefore, I do not fear.
The Lord is the strength of my life; intimidation has no power
over me.
(Psalm 27:1, NKJV)

God is with me. He strengthens me. He helps me.
He upholds me by His righteous right hand.
(Isaiah 41:10, NKJV)

I am strong and courageous. I am not afraid or dismayed,
because the Lord my God goes with me and will not leave me nor
forsake me.
(Deuteronomy 31:6, NKJV)

TROUBLE IS EXPECTED — FEAR IS NOT

I may face tribulation in this world, but I remain confident
because Christ has already overcome the world.
(John 16:33, NKJV)

God is my refuge and my strength—my very present help in
trouble.
Therefore, I will not fear.
(Psalm 46:1–2, NKJV)

FEAR IS NOT FROM GOD

God has not given me a spirit of fear,
but of power, love, and a sound mind.
Fear has no legal authority over my thoughts or decisions.
(2 Timothy 1:7, NKJV)

Perfect love drives out fear,
because fear involves torment—and torment has no place in me.
(1 John 4:18, NKJV)

GOD'S PRESENCE CANCELS INTIMIDATION

I am commanded to be strong and courageous.
I am not afraid or dismayed, because the Lord my God is with me
wherever I go.
(Joshua 1:9, NKJV)

Even when I walk through the valley of the shadow of death,
I fear no evil—because God is with me.
His presence comforts and secures me.
(Psalm 23:4, NKJV)

I am strong. I do not fear. I am not anxious.
My God comes with vengeance and salvation—He will save me.
(Isaiah 35:4, NKJV)

I BELONG TO GOD — FEAR HAS NO CLAIM

I belong to the Lord. I am redeemed and called by name.
Fear has no claim over what God has claimed as His own.
(Isaiah 43:1, NKJV)

When I pass through waters, I am not overwhelmed.
When I walk through fire, I am not burned.

God's presence preserves me through every trial.
(Isaiah 43:2, NKJV)

MY PEACE IS DIVINELY PROVIDED

Jesus has given me His peace—not the kind the world gives.
My heart is not troubled, and fear does not rule me.
(John 14:27, NKJV)

God keeps me in perfect peace
because my mind is stayed on Him and anchored in trust.
(Isaiah 26:3, NKJV)

FEAR IS DISPLACED BY TRUST

Whenever fear attempts to rise, I choose to trust in the Lord.
Trust governs my response—not panic or retreat.
(Psalm 56:3, NKJV)

The Lord is my helper. He will never leave me nor forsake me.
Therefore, I will not fear what man can do to me.
(Hebrews 13:5–6, NKJV)

I LIVE UNDER DIVINE COVERING

I dwell in the secret place of the Most High
and abide under the shadow of the Almighty.
The Lord is my refuge, my fortress, and my God—in Him I trust.
(Psalm 91:1–2, NKJV)

DAILY ALIGNMENT DECLARATION

The Lord is my light and my salvation.
Fear has no authority over me.

I expect challenges, but I do not submit to fear.
God has given me power, love, and a sound mind.

I receive the peace of Christ.
My mind is stayed on God.
My heart is anchored in truth.
I walk forward unafraid.

HOW TO USE THIS PRESCRIPTION

- Read daily
- Speak aloud when fear rises
- Return to it before decisions
- Use it to reset alignment, not emotion

Fear is not cured by reassurance.
It is cured by truth consistently applied.

You are not without peace.
You are not without power.
You are not without protection.

This prescription works—every time alignment is maintained.

About the Author ————————————

Dr. Joke Solanke is a trained healthcare professional, minister, and author whose work is shaped by years of direct patient care and ministerial service.

Through her work in primary and preventive care, Dr. Solanke has encountered many patients who initially present with physical concerns fatigue, chronic symptoms, weight management challenges, or general wellness issues only for deeper emotional and psychological struggles to surface over time. In many cases, fear, anxiety, unresolved stress, or trauma manifest physically long before they are consciously acknowledged.

Alongside her clinical work, Dr. Solanke's ministerial experience has revealed the same pattern in spiritual settings: individuals functioning outwardly while silently burdened inwardly. Whether in examination rooms or ministry spaces, she has observed how emotional and spiritual distress is often hidden beneath acceptable explanations, reinforced by denial, performance, or belief systems that discourage honest inner awareness.

Her combined clinical and ministerial experience has revealed a consistent truth: mental, emotional, and spiritual burdens are deeply interconnected with physical health. When these inner realities remain unaddressed, symptoms persist even when treatment is applied.

Rx for Fear emerges from these real-world encounters. It reflects a conviction shaped through practice rather than theory that lasting healing requires addressing the whole person: body, mind, and spirit. Rather than treating symptoms in isolation, Dr. Solanke invites readers into a process of restoration rooted in truth, alignment, and freedom from fear.

www.ingramcontent.com/pod-product-compliance
Lightning Source LLC
Chambersburg PA
CBHW070035100426
42740CB00013B/2695